W9-BSX-669

Modern Russian Poets on poetry

Edited by **CARL R. PROFFER**
Selected and Introduced by **JOSEPH BRODSKY**

Translated by
ALEXANDER GOLUBOV
JANE GARY HARRIS
DAVID LAPEZA
ANGELA LIVINGSTONE
JOEL STERN

Ardis / Ann Arbor

TABLE OF CONTENTS

PREFACE

Poetry has more in common with criticism than criticism with poetry, something confirmed by this book. Poetic thinking, which is called metaphorical, is in fact synthetic thinking. As such it contains analysis, but cannot be reduced to analysis. Analysis is neither the only nor the final form of cognition. There is also cognition through revelation, and there is cognition through meditation. Moreover, there is cognition through synthesis. In the case of the poet it is through intuitive synthesis, i.e., when the poet—according to the poet—steals left and right and does not even experience a sense of guilt as he does so.

Synthesis, as such, is not a parallel stage (degree) of relations with reality: it is the *following* stage. Intuitive synthesis, in its turn, is the next level up, if not the highest, a level whereon, in his relations to reality (in this case the poet) is guided by considerations not so much defined by it as dictated—sometimes literally—from without.

One of the dictating voices located outside of reality is language—or, more precisely, the harmonic element of language, which is better known publicly as the Muse. How this voice dictates is basically not important; what is important is that it dictates synthetic judgments which, according to Kant at least, are judgments wherein the predicate adds to the subject something which is not contained within the subject alone.

Let us add to this that one of the goals of synthesis is harmony. Let us add also that the poem "is a kind of harmonic whole." Translated into simple human terms this means that analysis is always a profile, synthesis is always *en face*, and a good poem is always stereoscopic.

What has been said, I should think, is sufficient to convince the reader if not of the superiority of poetic thinking to purely critical thinking, at least of the legitimacy of the poet's judgments about his art and the goals of this art. The virtue of this kind of judgment is not in its being "firsthand," but in the element of distancing which is essential before such a judgment can be uttered. The ability to distance is a unique thing in general, but in the case of the poet (and especially the poets presented in this anthology), it also indicates the scale on which his consciousness is working. In the case of the poet, distancing is not "one more boundary," it is a going beyond the boundary. The stereoscope takes on the qualities of the telescope. Imagine a person who gives confession while thinking about the phenomenon of giving confession.

This book has one other virtue compared to ordinary literary scholarship. As a rule, discussions of the nature of art are not very economical. But poetic thought, as we know,   is a diagonal,   i.e., the shortest—stylistic—distance between two points (the surrounding sentence). Tautology is the sin which is least characterisitic of poetry. Thus the essays in this anthology are extremely functional stylistically and represent (especially in the case of Mandelstam, Tsvetaeva, and Pasternak) the highest accomplishments of 20th-century Russian prose.

The late Auden said that the poet, unlike God, creates on the basis of experience. Said about the immanent creative process these words are equally applicable to the essays on poetic creation which are presented here; they are essays which were written on the basis of creative experience. However, one should certainly not regard this book as a collection of poetic credos: the poet expresses his true credo only in his poems. A poet turning to prose (something usually dictated by economic considerations, "dry spells," or more rarely, by polemical necessity) is like the shift from full gallop to trot, a time-exposure photograph of a monument, or Apollo's one year's service as shepherd for the flocks of King Admetus.

In other words, a poet's turning to prose is the tribute of dynamism to the stasis which preceded it; only the latter gains anything from such a switch: there is communicated to it a certain element of motion, which from the point of view of stasis looks like an acceleration, but which in the eyes of dynamism is only one of the forms of inertia. Prose and logic are the benefactors when Pegasus folds his wings, but not for long, because suddenly they experience a very strong temptation to move. It is for the sake of this temptation that this anthology has been compiled.

—Joseph Brodsky

Seven Twentieth-Century Russian Poets:
A Bio-bibliographical Introduction

All of the poets represented in this anthology are poets of very high stature. Indeed, excepting Gumilev, any of them could conceivably be called the greatest Russian poet of this century. The essays are among the best known by each poet. The third criterion for selection was that the essays deal with problems of general interest to poets and readers of poetry everywhere. Many excellent Russian essays of exclusively intra-mural interest were excluded, as were scholarly essays (Anna Akhmatova's works on Pushkin) or essays so dependent on their original linguistic form that meaningful translations could not be made. For all these reasons the anthology is not comprehensive. The absence of such poets as Akhmatova, Velimir Khlebnikov, Mikhail Kuzmin, and Nikolai Zabolotsky is regrettable but reasonable.

It is assumed that the average reader of *Modern Russian Poets on Poetry* will not know much about Russian literature, and that he will be encountering many of these writers for the first time. Therefore the notes which follow provide brief biographies, as well as bibliographies of English-language sources and translations. The annotation of each individual essay (see notes at the end of this volume) was also done with the non-specialist reader in mind. My goal was to prevent specific allusions from standing in the way of understanding of general problems.

This anthology was not planned with the idea that Pushkin would be its hero. But it has turned out that way, a fact which says much about the inevitability of Pushkin's importance for Russian poets. The virtual unanimity of Russian poets' respect for Pushkin is not understood in the English-speaking world; and given the impossibility of translating him, Pushkin's genius is something that has to be accepted on faith.

The bio-bibliographical information which follows is arranged in the order of the poets' appearance in the anthology, with a special section on Pushkin at the end.

Carl R. Proffer
University of Michigan

NIKOLAI GUMILEV (1886-1921)

Gumilev was born in Tsarskoe Selo, near St. Petersburg, attended the *gymnasium* there, and published his first book of poems *(The Path of Conquistadores)* in 1905. His first three or four books were rather derivative (especially of Symbolist and Decadent poets), but received some good reviews. He became one of the leading figures in the Guild of Poets (begun in 1911) and the movement known as Acmeism (or Clarism, or Adamism), one of several schools born out of the warm ashes of Symbolism. The Acmeists emphasized referential clarity and formal precision. Craftsmanship and comprehensibility are virtues praised by Gumilev in his critical writing.

Gumilev married Anna Akhmatova in 1910, but they were divorced in 1918. During that time Gumilev published widely (poetry and essays on poetry), travelled to Africa twice, enlisted in the army in 1914, and was repeatedly decorated for valor in battle. Though a monarchist, he returned from Paris to Russia after the Bolshevik coup and engaged in teaching and translating. In 1921 he was arrested and shot—for alleged involvement in an anti-Soviet plot.

Gumilev's last, and best, book—*Pillar of Fire*—was published in 1921, and he has not been published in the USSR since the early 1920s. Most of his criticism was collected in a Russian volume in 1923; all of it was published in the four-volume emigre edition of his works [*Sobranie sochinenii* (Washington, D. C., 1962-68)]. Many of the writings on poetry are available in English in Nikolai Gumilev, *On Russian Poetry* (see Bibliography).

OSIP MANDELSTAM (1891-1938)

Born in Warsaw of Jewish parents, Mandelstam grew up in St. Petersburg and Tsarskoe Selo. Friendship with Gumilev led him to join the Guild of Poets and Acmeism. His first book was *Stone* (1913), his most important book *Tristia* (1922). But much of his best work was not even published in his lifetime. Ideological incompatability made it increasingly difficult for him to survive in the 1920s. However, he did continue writing poetry, prose, and criticism. Some of the most striking prose was published in 1928 in his book *The Egyptian Stamp.* He was repeatedly arrested and exiled in the Thirties, and finally died in a Siberian labor camp in 1938. The details of his life are recorded in two monumental memoirs by his wife, Nadezhda Mandelstam: *Hope Against Hope* and *Hope Abandoned.*

Mandelstam has come to be regarded as one of the greatest of all

Russian poets. Thematically and formally there is a strong classical inclination in his lyrics, particularly during his early, or Acmeist, period. Later his poems are often more visionary, reflections of cultural and psychological disintegration.

Although officially "rehabilitated" during the so-called thaw after Stalin's death, Mandelstam is still seldom published in the Soviet Union; and the only significant collection of his works was published in the United States [*Sobranie sochinenii*, 3 volumes (Washington, D.C., 1967-69)], and the major Mandelstam archive is now at Princeton University.

ALEXANDER BLOK (1880-1921)

Reared in a rarefied atmosphere of artistocratic arts, Blok became the most revered poet of St. Petersburg Symbolism. His first book was *Ante Lucem* (1898-1900); it was followed by the hazy but mellifluous *Verse about The Beautiful Lady* (1901-1902). Along with his friend and fellow Symbolist, Andrei Bely, he made a cult of the Divine Sophia, a theological lucubration of philosopher Vladimir Solovyov. Over the years Blok's image of this feminine muse changed from vague, joyous, gold and shining to clear, harlot-like and destructive. But Blok remained the leading poet of the period, a regular fixture in all Symbolist publications. Therefore Blok did not seem a likely candidate to write what would become known as *the* poem of the 1917 Revolution—"The Twelve" (1918). Along with his lyrics it remains his best known work, and it has been subjected to many different interpretations.

Basically Blok is a poet of the "old world"—turn-of-the-century Russia with her last flowering of art, ballet, music and poetry. After Blok's age silver spoons were no longer part of the delivery-room equipment. Blok did engage in social activity after 1917, working on various committees, teaching and translating—but it seems his heart was not in it, and that in some measure his early death was due to the passing of the Silver Age. —The selection printed in this anthology was Blok's last public speech.

VLADISLAV KHODASEVICH (1886-1939)

His mother was a Jew, his father a Polish Catholic. He began his literary career in Moscow, but a few years in Petrograd (the new name for St. Petersburg) were crucial in his development, and in his decision to emigrate from the new Russia. Khodasevich's first two books of poems are considered apprenticeship volumes *(Youth,* 1908; *A Happy Little House,* (1914). *The Way of Grain* (1920) begins his mature period, and, as Vladimir Nabokov puts it (for a number of connoisseurs) "there are few things in modern world poetry comparable to the poems of his *Heavy Lyre"* (1922). In his brevity and precision Khodasevich is one of the few true descendants of Pushkin in Russian lyric poetry. And Pushkin was his hero, subject of several essays, including the selection in this volume.

After the Revolution Khodasevich survived by doing the usual "social work" demanded of writers (lectures to worker writers, etc.) and by living in Petrograd's House of Writers (1919-22), set up by Gorky. With Nina Berberova he emigrated in June 1922, travelling first to Berlin, then wandering for a while before settling in Paris in 1925. He wrote for many emigre periodicals, mainly reviews and essays. He finished a book on the eighteenth-century poet Derzhavin. But he wrote relatively little poetry, and he made many powerful literary enemies because of his wit and his principles.

Khodasevich did not expect fame in his lifetime. In unpublished diaries kept during the Civil War he wrote that his poetry would really come to be valued only at a point so far in the future that only the subtlest experts would be able to tell his language from that of Mayakovsky—which is roughly equivalent to being unable to distinguish Robert Frost from Vachel Lindsay.

BORIS PASTERNAK (1890-1960)

Pasternak was born and died a Muscovite, the first son of a well known artist and a concert pianist, both Jews. His early passion for music, Scriabine particularly, gave way to philosophy and poetry. He studied in Germany (see his autobiography *Safe Conduct),* then graduated from Moscow University. He became friends with Mayakovsky, and in the early part of his career was associated with the Futurists—though he is not usually discussed in histories of Futurism. His second book, *Above the Barriers* (1917) was published by Centrifuge, the Futurist publishing house. But his most famous collections are the next two: *My Sister, Life* (published in 1922) and *Themes and Variations* (1923). The dense intercuttings of imagery and the harsh consonantal diction were as innovative as anything the Futurists did, but simultaneously the poems made it clear that he was

13

an integral part of the classical traditions in Russian verse. He also wrote a number of stories and memoirs, often thinking of a novel. Much of what he wrote both then and later still remains unpublished, the most complete edition of his works in Russian being the four-volume set published by the University of Michigan Press in the 1960s.

Pasternak's family emigrated after the Bolshevik Revolution, but he remained to the end. He was printed rather infrequently during the rest of his life, even though he sometimes did things which might placate the new regime—writing on acceptable themes (his long poem about the revolutionary hero, *Lieutenant Schmidt* [1926]) and, later, translating some of Stalin's poems from Georgian. More importantly, he translated—often quite freely—*Faust* and many of Shakespeare's plays. Pasternak was never arrested, but when his novel *Doctor Zhivago* was published abroad in 1958 and he won the Nobel Prize, a vicious public campaign against him began. He was denounced by the Soviet Union of Writers and forced to decline the award. He died a year later.

Pasternak shares with Tsvetaeva, among the authors in this volume, prose which is impossible to translate adequately, and a style dominated less by clear logic than metaphor, paradox, and ellipsis.

VLADIMIR MAYAKOVSKY (1893-1930)

Mayakovsky was born in Georgia, the son of a forester; his family moved to Moscow when he was thirteen. By the fall of 1909 he had been arrested three times for revolutionary activities and spent seven months in jails. Painting school led him to meet David Burlyuk (1882-1967) and eventually to play a major role in the foundation of Russian Futurism in the years 1910-13. Flamboyance, scandal and good-humored vulgarity marked the early years of the movement. Among Mayakovsky's best known early works are the long poems *Vladimir Mayakovsky* (1914), *A Cloud in Trousers* (1915), and *The Backbone Flute* (1916). In his poetry rejection of classical Russian culture—and (what was regarded as) the mush of Symbolism—led to the destruction of most poetic conventions: meter, rhyme, rhythm, graphic arrangement, diction and imagery. His no-nonsense pragmatism and his ideological utilitarianism are clear in "How to Make Verse."

After the revolutions of 1917 he devoted himself to The Cause wholeheartedly, even doing advertising jingles for baby-bottle nipples and Bolshevik propaganda. He founded the journal *LEF* (Left Front of the Arts, 1923) and its successor, *New LEF*. Because of Party politics, and his own formidable individualism, he was often involved in polemics. Major long poems of the period are *Vladimir Ilych Lenin* (1925) and *It's Good* (1927). Mayakovsky shot himself to death in 1930. This was five years after Esenin's suicide, which plays such a major part in the essay printed below. The reasons for Mayakovsky's suicide have not been fully disclosed, but character, romance, and politics probably all were important.

MARINA TSVETAEVA (1892-1941)

Tsvetaeva's mother, who gave up a career as a pianist to marry, put all her musical hopes on her daughter. She was given an excellent education in the arts, attended boarding schools in France and Germany, and graduated from a Moscow high school. She began publishing privately in 1910, and became acquainted with many of the leading writers of the day, including Mandelstam and Akhmatova. She tended to have crushes on writers, both living and dead ones, and of both sexes; all through her career she had periods of hero-worship (Rostand, Rilke, Napoleon, Akhmatova, Mayakovsky), often reflected in the subject matter of her poems. Her early reputation was established by the collection *Landmarks* (1916-22).

During the Civil War she lived in great poverty, caring for the poet Balmont, and separated from her husband—a White soldier who would become, years later, a Soviet assassin. Tsvetaeva emigrated to Berlin in 1921, and lived in Paris from 1925 to 1939. Here too she lived in dire poverty, with her children. Her poetry continued to evolve; she did many formal experiments, while remaining essentially classical (when compared to the Futurists). The variety of her themes, genres and styles makes it difficult to generalize about her work. The elliptical style of the selection presented in this volume is typical of her poetry and prose, much of which is just now being published.

In 1939 Tsvetaeva returned to the Soviet Union, where her eldest daughter was in a prison camp and her estranged husband was being executed. Tsvetaeva found little welcome in Moscow, no place to live, and she was soon forced to leave. After a short, dismal period in the small town of Elabuga, she hanged herself.

15

BIBLIOGRAPHY

The notes at the end of this volume contain many references to useful translations and criticism of writers mentioned in the essays, as well as suggested articles and books on general topics such as Symbolism, Acmeism, and Futurism. Generally, this bibliography does not duplicate these references. This first section contains anthologies of poetry in which the seven authors of *Modern Russian Poets on Poetry* are featured, and general studies of modern Russian poetry. In the second part of the bibliography the reader will find translations of, as well as biographical and critical works about, each of the seven authors—in the order in which they appear in this volume. At the end are suggested translations and criticism of Pushkin.

General Anthologies and Criticism

Vladimir Markov and Merril Sparks, (eds.), *Modern Russian Poetry*. Indianapolis: Bobbs-Merrill, 1966.
A. Yarmolinsky, (ed.), *Two Centuries of Russian Verse*. New York: Random House, 1966.
Olga Carlisle, (ed.), *Poets on Street Corners*. New York: Random House, 1968.
Dmitri Obolensky, *The Penguin Book of Russian Verse*. Baltimore: Penguin, 1962,65.
    Reprinted as *The Heritage of Russian Verse* by Indiana University Press, 1976.
C. M. Bowra, *A Second Book of Russian Verse*. London, 1948.

Vahan Barooshian, *Russian Cubo-Futurism 1910-30*. The Hague: Mouton, 1974.
Christopher Barnes, (ed.), *Studies in Twentieth-Century Russian Literature*. New York: Barnes & Noble, 1976.
E. J. Brown, (ed.), *Major Soviet Writers*. Oxford University Press, 1973.
George Gibian & W. Tjalsma, (eds.), *Russian Modernism: Culture and the Avant-Garde 1900-30*. Ithaca: Cornell University Press, 1976.
A. Kaun, *Soviet Poets and Poetry*. Berkeley: University of California Press, 1943.
R. Poggioli, *The Poets of Russia 1890-1930*. Harvard University Press, 1960.

Nikolai Gumilev

Translations

Selected Works of Nikolai S. Gumilev, trans. Burton Raffel & Alla Burago, introduction by Sydney Monas. Albany: SUNY Press, 1972.
Nikolai Gumilev, *On Russian Poetry,* trans. David Lapeza. Ann Arbor: Ardis, 1976.

Nikolai Gumilev, "Symbolism's Legacy and Acmeism," *Russian Literature Triquarterly,* No. 1 (1971), 139-44. Preface and translation by R. Whittaker.

Criticism

Leonid Strakhovsky, *Craftsmen of the Word. Three Poets of Modern Russia: Gumilev, Akhmatova, Mandelstam.* Westport, Conn: Greenwood Press, 1969.

Earl Sampson, "Nikolai Gumilev: Toward a Reevaluation," *The Russian Review,* XXIX, 2 (1970).

Earl Sampson, "In the Middle of the Journey of Life: Gumilev's *Pillar of Fire,"* *Russian Literature Triquarterly,* No. 1 (1971), 283-96.

Sam Driver, "Acmeism," *Slavic and East European Journal,* XII, 2 (1968), 141-56.

OSIP MANDELSTAM

Translations

The Complete Critical Prose and Letters. Ed. & trans. Jane Gary Harris & Constance Anthony. Ann Arbor: Ardis, 1976.

The Prose of Osip Mandelstam. Ed. & trans. Clarence Brown. Princeton University Press, 1965.

Complete Poetry of Osip Mandelstam. Trans. Burton Raffel & Alla Burago. Albany: SUNY Press, 1973. *[NB. The translations in this volume are extremely unreliable and should be used only when others—see the next entries—do not exist.]*

Selected Poems. Bilingual edition, trans. David McDuff. New York: Noonday, 1975.

Selected Poems. Trans. Clarence Brown and W. S. Merwin. New York: Atheneum, 1974.

Tristia, trans. Bruce McClelland, in *The Silver Age of Russian Culture,* ed. Carl and Ellendea Proffer. Ann Arbor: Ardis, 1975. pp. 159-99.

Criticism

Clarence Brown, *Mandelstam.* Cambridge University Press, 1973.

Nadezhda Mandelstam, *Hope Against Hope.* New York: Atheneum, 1970. Paperback edition, 1976.

Nadezhda Mandelstam, *Hope Abandoned.* New York: Atheneum, 1974.

Nadezhda Mandelstam, *Mozart and Salieri: An Essay on the Poetry of Mandelstam.* Ann Arbor: Ardis, 1973.

Arthur A. Cohen, *Osip Emilevich Mandelstam: An Essay in Antiphon.* Ann Arbor: Ardis, 1974.

Donald Rayfield, "Mandelstam's Voronezh Poetry," *Russian Literature Triquarterly,* No. 11 (1975), 323-63.

Boris Bukhshtab, "The Poetry of Mandelstam," *Russian Literature Triquarterly,* No. 1 (1971), 262-82.

Alexander Blok

Translations

"The Twelve," "Nightingale Garden," "The Unknown Lady," and other poems, in *The Silver Age of Russian Culture,* ed. Carl and Ellendea Proffer. Ann Arbor, 1975. pp. 77-113.
The Spirit of Music, trans. I. Freiman. London: L. Drummond, 1946.
The Journey to Italy, trans. Lucy Vogel. Ithaca: Cornell University Press, 1973.

Criticism

F. D. Reeve, *Alexander Blok.* New York: Columbia University Press, 1962.
Kornei Chukovsky, *Alexander Blok.* [In press, Ann Arbor: Ardis, 1977].
Oleg Maslennikov, *The Frenzied Poets.* Berkeley: University of California Press, 1952.
C. M. Bowra, *The Heritage of Symbolism.* London, 1951.
G. Donchin, *The Influence of French Symbolism on Russian Poetry.* The Hague, 1958.
V. Erlich, "The Maker and the Seer: Two Russian Symbolists," *The Double Image.* Baltimore: Johns Hopkins Press, 1964.
Munir Sendich, "Blok's *The Twelve:* Critical Interpretations of the Christ Figure, with a Bibliography of Criticism 1918-70," *Russian Literature Triquarterly,* No. 4 (1972), pp. 445-72.

Vladislav Khodasevich

Translations

"The Monkey," "Poem," "Orpheus," trans. Vladimir Nabokov. *TriQuarterly,* No. 27 (Spring 1973), 67-70.
"Thirty-four lyric poems of Khodasevich," trans. Alexander Landman. *Russian Literature Triquarterly,* No. 8 (1974), 45-64.
"Tolstoy's Departure," trans. Elizabeth Shephard. *TriQuarterly,* No. 27 (1973), 71-82.

Criticism

Nina Berberova, *The Italics Are Mine.* New York: Harcourt, Brace, 1969.
Vladimir Nabokov, "On Khodasevich," *TriQuarterly,* No. 27 (1973), 83-87.
Robert Hughes, "Khodasevich: Irony and Dislocation: A Poet in Exile," *ibid.,* 52-66.
Vladimir Markov, "Georgy Ivanov: Nihilist as Light-bearer," *ibid.,* 139-53.
Wladimir Weidle, "A Double-edged *Ars Poetica,*" *Russian Literature Triquarterly,* No. 2 (1972), 338-47.
Nina Berberova, "Vladislav Khodasevich—A Russian Poet," *The Russian Review,* XI (1952), 78-85.

Boris Pasternak

Translations

The Poetry of Boris Pasternak, trans. George Reavey. New York: Putnam's, 1959.

Fifty Poems, trans. Lydia Pasternak Slater. London: Allen & Unwin, 1963.

Doctor Zhivago, trans. Max Hayward and M. Harari. New York: Pantheon, 1958

The Poems of Doctor Zhivago, trans. with commentary by Donald Davie. New York: Barnes and Noble, 1965.

The Collected Prose Works, ed. S. Schimanski. London: Lindsay Drummond, 1945.

An Essay in Autobiography, trans. Manya Harari. London: Collins, 1959.

Criticism

Donald Davie and Angela Livingstone, (eds.), Pasternak: Modern Judgements. Nashville, Tenn.: Aurora Publishers, 1970.

Olga Hughes, The Poetic World of Boris Pasternak. Princeton University Press, 1974.

J. W. Dyck, Boris Pasternak. New York: Twayne, 1972.

Dale Plank, Pasternak's Lyric: A Study of Sound and Imagery. The Hague: Mouton, 1966.

Gleb Struve, "Sense and Nonsense about Doctor Zhivago," in Studies in Russian and Polish Literature, ed. Z. Folejewski. The Hague, 1962.

Jane Gary Harris, "Pasternak's Vision of Life: The History of a Feminine Image," Russian Literature Triquarterly, No. 9 (1974), 389-422.

Vladimir Mayakovsky

Translations

The Bedbug and Selected Poetry, ed. Pat Blake, trans. M. Hayward and G. Reavey. Bloomington: Indiana University Press, 1975.

"Man," trans. Gary Wiggins. Russian Literature Triquarterly, No. 12 (1975), 37-63.

The Complete Plays of Mayakovsky, trans. Guy Daniels. New York, 1968.

Poems, trans. Dorian Rottenberg. Moscow: Progress Publishers, 1972.

Criticism

Wiktor Woroszylski, The Life of Mayakovsky. New York: Grossman, 1970.

E. J. Brown, Mayakovsky. Princeton University Press, 1973.

Bengt Jangfeldt, Mayakovsky and Futurism 1917-21. Stockholm: Almqvist and Wiksell, 1976.

Viktor Shklovsky, Mayakovsky and His Circle. New York: Dodd, Mead, 1972.

Russian Literature Triquarterly, No. 12 and No. 13 (1975-1976), "Russian Futurism and Constructivism," Parts I and II.

Roman Jakobson, "On a Generation that Squandered its Poets," in E. J. Brown, ed. Major Soviet Writers, Oxford University Press, 1973. pp. 7-32.

C. M. Bowra, "The Futurism of Vladimir Mayakovsky," *The Creative Experiment*. New York: Grove, n.d., pp. 94-127.

Marina Tsvetaeva

Translations

Poems of Tsvetaeva, trans. E. Fenn. London, 1973.
"To Mayakovsky," "Psyche," "Poems grow like stars," trans. Paul Schmidt. *TriQuarterly,* No. 27 (1973), 94-102.
Nine lyric poems, trans. Jamie Fuller and George Kline. *Russian Literature Triquarterly,* No. 2 (1972), 214-20.
Eight lyric poems, trans. Lydia Pasternak Slater, and Angela Livingstone. *Russian Literature Triquarterly,* No. 9 (1974), 21-24.
"Mother and Music," trans. Janet King. *Russian Literature Triquarterly,* No. 11 (1975), 29-50.
"A Poet on Criticism," trans. Paul Schmidt. *TriQuarterly,* No. 27 (1973), 103-134.

Criticism

Simon Karlinsky, *Marina Tsvetaeva*. Berkeley: Univ. of California Press, 1966.
Angela Livingstone, "Tsvetaeva's 'Art in the Light of Conscience'," *Russian Literature Triquarterly,* No. 11 (1975), 363-79.
Jane Taubman, "Tsvetaeva and Akhmatova," *Russian Literature Triquarterly,* No. 9 (1974), 355-70.
Jane Taubman, "Tsvetaeva and Pasternak: Toward the History of a Friendship," *Russian Literature Triquarterly,* No. 2 (1972), 303-322.
D. S. Mirsky, "Marina Tsvetaeva," *TriQuarterly,* No. 27 (1973), 88-93.

Alexander Pushkin

Translations

Eugene Onegin, translated, with commentaries by Vladimir Nabokov. Bollingen Series, Pantheon Books, 1964 (4 volumes); revised edition by Princeton University Press, 1975.
John Fennell, ed., *The Penguin Pushkin.* Penguin Books, 1964.
Walter Arndt, trans., *Pushkin Threefold.* New York: Dutton, 1972.
Walter Arndt, trans., *Ruslan and Ludmila.* Ann Arbor: Ardis, 1974.
Carl R. Proffer, trans., *The Critical Prose of Alexander Pushkin.* Bloomington: Indiana University Press, 1969.
G. Aitken, trans., *The Complete Prose Tales of Pushkin.* London: Barrie, 1965.

Criticism

Walter Vickery, *Alexander Pushkin.* New York: Twayne, 1970.
Ernest J. Simmons, *Alexander Pushkin.* New York: Vintage, 1964.
D. S. Mirsky, *Pushkin.* New York: Dutton, 1963.

MODERN RUSSIAN POETS ON POETRY

Nikolai Gumilev

THE LIFE OF VERSE

I

The peasant plows, the stonemason builds, the priest prays and the judge judges. What does the poet do? Why does he not set forth in easily memorized verses the sprouting of various grasses, why does he refuse to compose a new popular song such as "Dubinushka" or sweeten the bitter medicine of religious theses? Why is it that only in moments of faint-heartedness will he admit that he aroused good feelings with his lyre? Does the poet really have no place in society, no matter whether among the bourgeoisie, the social democrats, or in the religious community? Let John the Damascene be silent!

Thus say the champions of the thesis "Art for Life." Hence —François Coppée, Sully-Prudhomme, Nekrasov, and in many ways, Andrei Bely.

The defenders of "Art for Art's Sake" retort: "Go away, what does the peaceful poet have to do with you... you offend his soul, like coffins, you've still got whips, dungeons, and axes to defend your stupidity and malice, enough of you, mad slaves... For us, Princes of Song, sovereigns of the castles of dreams, life is merely a means of flight: the harder a dancer strikes the earth with his feet, the higher he soars. Whether we chase our verses like goblets, or write obscure, virtually drunken ditties, we are always, and primarily, free, and we have utterly no desire to be useful."

Hence—Hérédia, Verlaine, and in our country, Maikov.

This controversy will go on for many more centuries, without leading to any results, and this is not surprising, for of any attitude toward anything, whether it be toward people, things, or ideas, we require above all that it be chaste. By this I mean the right of every phenomenon to be valuable in itself,

23

not to require justification of its existence and some other, higher right to serve others.

Homer sharpened his hexameters, unconcerned with anything except vowel and consonant sounds, caesurae and spondees, and adapted his content to them. However, he would have considered himself a poor craftsman if, hearing his songs, youths had not striven for martial glory, if the misty gaze of young girls had not increased the beauty of peace.

Unchasteness of attitude is present in both the doctrine of "Art for Life" and that of "Art for Art's Sake."

In the first case art is brought down to the level of a prostitute or a soldier. Its existence has value only to the extent that it serves goals extraneous to it. It would not be surprising if the eyes of the gentle muses were to grow dull, and they developed bad manners.

In the second case art becomes effete, grows agonizingly moony, Mallarmé's words, put in the mouth of his *Hérodiade*, are applicable to it:

> ...*J'aime l'horreur d'être vierge et je veux*
> *Vivre parmi l'effroi que me font mes cheveux...*

> (I love the horror of being virgin and I want/
> to live amidst the terror my hair inspires...)

Purity is suppressed sensuality, and it is beautiful; the absence of sensuality is frightening, like a new unheard-of form of depravity.

No! cries the era of aesthetic puritanism, of great demands on the poet as creator, on idea or word as artistic material. The poet must place upon himself the fetters of difficult forms (recall Homer's hexameters, Dante's terze rime and sonnets, the Old Scottish stanzas of Byron's poems) or ordinary forms, but in a stage of advanced development, brought to the point of impossibility (Pushkin's iambs), he must do this—but only in praise of his God, whom he is obliged to have. Otherwise he would be a simple gymnast.

Still, if I were to choose between the two above doctrines, I would say that in the first there is greater respect for art and understanding of its essence. There is a new aim imposed upon it, a new application is indicated for the powers boiling within it, an unworthy, low application perhaps—that is not important: isn't the cleaning of the Augean stables referred to on an equal basis with the other great feats of Hercules? In ancient ballads it is told that Roland was depressed when a dozen enemies rode out against him. He could fight beautifully and worthily only against hundreds. However, one should not forget that even Roland could be defeated.

Now I shall speak only of poetry, recalling Oscar Wilde's words, which horrified the weak and inspired courage in the strong: "For the material that the painter or sculptor uses is meagre in comparison with that of words. Words have not merely music as sweet as that of viol and lute, color as rich and vivid as any that makes lovely for us the canvas of the Venetian or the Spaniard, and plastic form no less sure and certain than that which reveals itself in marble or in bronze, but thought and passion and spirituality are theirs also, are theirs, indeed, alone."

And, that verse is the highest form of speech is known to everyone who, carefully sharpening a piece of prose, used force to restrain the rising rhythm.

II

The origin of separate poems is mysteriously akin to the origin of living organisms. The poet's thought receives a shock from the external world, sometimes in an unforgettably clear moment, sometimes dimly, like conception in sleep, and for a long time it is necessary to bear the foetus of the future creation, heeding the timid movements of the still weak new life. Everything affects the course of its development—a beam of the horned moon, an unexpectedly heard melody, a book read, a flower's smell. Everything determines its future fate. The ancients respected the silent poet, as one respects a woman preparing to be a mother.

Finally, in the labor, like the labor of childbirth (Turgenev speaks of this) a poem appears. It is lucky if, in the moment of its appearance, the poet is not distracted by some considerations extraneous to art, if, gentle as a dove, he strives to convey what was born at full term, finished, and tries, wise as a serpent, to include all this in the most perfect form.

Such a poem can live for centuries, moving from temporary oblivion to new glory, and even dead, will, like King Solomon, long inspire in men a sacred trembling. Such is the *Iliad*.

But there are poems not born at full term, in which, around the original impressions, others did not manage to accumulate, and there are those in which on the contrary details obscure the basic theme, they are cripples in the world of images, and the perfection of their separate parts does not gladden, but rather saddens us, like the beautiful eyes of hunchbacks. We are much obliged to hunchbacks, they tell us surprising things, but sometimes you dream with such longing of the svelte youths of Sparta, that you no longer pity their weak brothers and sisters, condemned by a severe law. This is what Apollo wants, a rather frightening, cruel, but terribly beautiful god.

What is necessary for a poem to live, and not in a jar of alcohol, like some curious freak, not the half-life of the invalid in a wheelchair, but a full and powerful life—for it to arouse love and hatred, to make the world reckon with the fact of its existence? What requirements must it satisfy?

I would answer in short: *all*.

Really, it must have: thought and feeling—without the first, the most lyrical poem will be dead, and without the second, even an epic ballad will appear a dull contrivance (Pushkin in his lyrics and Schiller in his ballads knew this),—the softness of outline of a young body, where nothing stands out, nothing is wasted, and the definition of a statue in sunlight; simplicity—only for it is the future open, and—refinement, as a living recognition of the continuity of all joys and sorrows of past ages; and above all that—style and gesture.

In style God appears from out his creation, the poet gives himself away, but the secret self, unknown even to him, and allows us to guess the color of his eyes, the shape of his hands. And that is so important. For we love Dante Alighieri, the boy in love with Beatrice's pallor of face, the frenzied Ghibelline and the Veronese exile, no less than his *Divine Comedy*... By gesture in a poem I mean such arrangement of words, choice of vowel and consonant sounds, acceleration and deceleration of rhythm as has the reader of the poem strike the pose of his hero, copy his mimicry and movements and, thanks to the suggestion of his own body, experience what the poet himself did, so that the spoken idea becomes no longer a lie, but the truth. Poets' complaints about the fact that the public does not sympathize with their sufferings, intoxicated with the music of verse, are based on misunderstanding. The joy, the sorrow, the despair the reader feels are only *his own*. To arouse sympathy, one must speak of oneself in a clumsy manner, as Nadson did.

I return to the preceding: to be worthy of its name, a poem, having the qualities enumerated, must preserve complete harmony among them and, what is most important, be called to life not "by irritation of a captive thought," but by internal necessity which gives it a living soul—a temperament. Besides that, it must be impeccable even to the point of irregularity. Because only conscious departures from the generally accepted norms give a poem individuality, though they love to disguise themselves as unconscious ones. Thus, Charles Asselineau tells of an "uncontrolled sonnet," where the author, consciously breaking the rules, pretends that he does it in a burst of poetic inspiration or a fit of passion. Ronsard, Maynard, Malherbe wrote such sonnets. These irregularities play the role of birthmarks, through them it is easiest of all to recall to mind the aspect of the whole.

In short, a poem must be a copy of the beautiful human body, that highest level of perfection imaginable: with reason did men create even the Lord God in their own image and likeness. Such a poem is valuable in itself, it has the right to exist at all costs. Thus to save one man expeditions are got ready in which dozens of other men perish. But, yet, once he is saved, he must, as everyone else, justify to himself his own existence.

27

Really, the world of images is in close connection with the
world of men, but not as people usually believe. Not being an
analogy of life, art does not have an existence completely like
ours, cannot convey to us a perceptible link with other realities.
Poems written even by true visionaries in moments of trance have
meaning only in so far as they are good. To think otherwise is to
repeat the famous mistake of the sparrows that wanted to peck
painted fruit.

But beautiful poems, like living beings, enter the circle of
our life; they now instruct, now appeal, now bless; among them
are guardian angels, wise leaders, tempter demons and dear
friends. Under their influence men love, hate and die. In many
respects they are the highest judges, like the totems of the North
American Indians. For example—Turgenev's "A Quiet Backwater," where the poem "The Upas Tree," by its strength and
distance, precipitates the dénouement of a solitary love, painful
in the Russian fashion; or—Dostoevsky's *The Idiot*, when "The
Poor Knight" resounds, like an incantation on Aglaya's lips, mad
with the craving to love the hero; or—Sologub's "Night Dances"
with their poet, enchanting willful princesses with the marvelous music of Lermontovian stanzas.

In contemporary Russian poetry, as an example of such
"living" poems, I will point out only a few, attempting only to
illustrate the above, and setting aside much that is important and
characteristic. Here, for example, is a poem by Valery Bryusov,
"In the Crypt":

You are laid out in the tomb in myrtle crown.
I kiss the moon's reflection on your face.

Through latticed windows the circle of the moon
                    is seen.
In the clear sky, as above us, the secret of silence.

Behind you at your pillow a wreath of damp roses,
On your eyes, like pearls, drops of former tears.

A moon beam, caressing the roses, silvers the pearls,
Moon light circles round the ancient marble slabs.

What do you see, what remember in your unwaking
sleep?
Dark shadows bend ever lower towards me.

I came to you into the tomb through the black garden.
By the doors lemurs watch maliciously over me.

I know, I know I won't be long alone with you!
The moon light completes its measured circle path.

You are motionless, you are beautiful, in myrtle crown.
I kiss the light of heaven on your face!

Here, in this poem, the Bryusovian passion, which allows him to treat even the higher terror of death, of disappearance, thoughtlessly, and the Bryusovian tenderness, a tenderness almost maidenly, which everything gladdens, everything torments, the moonbeams, the pearls, the roses—these two most characteristic qualities of his work help him to create an image, a copy perhaps, of the instant of meeting of lovers irrevocably separated and forever poisoned by this separation.

In the poem "The Heliads" *(Transparence,* p. 124) Vyacheslav Ivanov, the poet, through his sunniness and purely masculine power, so different from the lunar femininity of Bryusov, gives the image of Phaëthon. He transforms the bright ancient tale into eternally young truth. There have always been men condemned to perish by the very nature of their daring. But they did not always know that defeat could be more fruitful than victory.

He was beautiful, proud youth,
Son of the Sun, young Sun-god,

When he seized with firm hand
The fateful pledge of grandeur—

When from the blushing Horae,
He carried off the reins of his realm—
And the steeds struggled against the gates,
Smelling the flaming expanse!

And, freed, flew up, neighed,
Deserting the scarlet prison,
And ran with the clatter of brazen hoofs,
Obedient to the light yoke... etc.

The "proud youth" does not appear in the poem itself, but we see him in the words and songs of the three maiden Heliads, in love with him, pushing him toward his doom and mourning him "on the green Eridanus." And agonizingly enviable is the fate of one, of whom maidens sing such songs!

Innokenty Annensky is also mighty, but with a might that is not so much Manly as Human. In him feeling does not give birth to thought, as usually happens in poets, rather the thought itself grows so strong that it becomes feeling live even to the point of pain. He loves exclusively "today" and exclusively "here," and this love leads him not only to the pursuit of decoration, but of decorativeness. His verses suffer from this, they inflict upon the soul incurable wounds and one must fight against them with the spells of time and space.

What grave, dark delirium!
How turbid, moony these summits!
To touch violins so many years
And not recognize their strings in the light!

Who needs us? Who lit
Two yellow, two melancholy faces?
And suddenly felt their union,
That someone took and someone merged them.

Oh, how long ago! Through this darkness
Say one thing: —are you she, she?
And the strings fawned upon him,
Ringing, but, fawning, trembled.

Isn't it so? Never more
Shall we part—all right?
And the violin answers, "Yes,"
But the violin's heart ached.

The bow understood everything, it fell silent,
But in the violin the echo was sustained,
And it was torture for them,
What seemed music to men.

But the man did not put out
The light until morning...and the strings sang,
Only morning found them exhausted
On the black velvet of their bed.

To whom has this not happened? Who has not had to bend over their dream, feeling that the possibility of realizing it has been lost irrevocably? And he who, having read this poem, forgets the eternal, virginal freshness of the world, believes that there is only torment, even if it seems like music, he is lost, he is poisoned. But are we not captivated by the thought of death from such a melodious arrow?

Next, passing over Blok's "Lady"—there is so much written about her—I will say something about Kuzmin's *Chimes of Love*. At the same time, the author wrote music to them, and this placed upon them the mark of a certain special exaltation and elegance, accessible only to pure sounds. The verse flows, like a stream of thick, fragrant and sweet honey, you believe that it alone is the natural form of human speech, and conversation or a prose passage afterwards would seem somehow dreadful, like a whisper in the Tyutchevian night, like an unclean spell. This poem is composed of a series of lyrical passages, hymns to love and about love. Its words can be repeated every day, as you repeat a prayer, inhale the scent of perfume, look at flowers. I include one passage from it, which completely captivates our conception of tomorrow, makes it a cornucopia:

Love sets out nets
Of strongest silks;
Lovers, like children,
Look for chains.

Yesterday you know not love,
Today you're all aflame.
Yesterday you reject me,
Today vow to me.

Tomorrow the beloved will love
And the unbeloved yesterday,
He'll come to you who was not
Other evenings.

Love, who will love
When the time comes,
And what will be, will be,
What fate prepared us.

We, like little children,
Look for chains,
And blindly fall into the nets
Of strongest silks.

Thus art, born of life, approaches it again, but not as a cheap laborer, not as a peevish grumbler, but as an equal to an equal.

Translated by David Lapeza

Osip Mandelstam

ON THE NATURE OF THE WORD

> We have forgotten that the word alone
> Shone radiant over the troubled earth,
> And that in the Gospel of St. John
> It is written that the word is God.
> But we have limited its range
> To the paltry boundaries of this world,
> And like dead bees in an empty hive
> Dead words emit a foul odor.

N. Gumilev

I would like to pose one question: is Russian literature a unified whole? Is contemporary Russian literature in fact the selfsame thing as the literature of Nekrasov, Pushkin, Derzhavin or Simeon Polotsky? If continuity has been maintained, how far back does it go into the past? If Russian literature remains unchanged, what constitutes its unity, what is its essential principle (its so-called criterion for being)?

The question I have posed becomes particularly acute in view of the quickening tempo of the historical process. Of course, it is certainly an exaggeration to regard each year of contemporary history as a century, but something like a geometric progression, a regular and natural acceleration, is perceptible in the stormy realization of the already accumulated and still-increasing potential of historical energy. Due to the quantitative change in the content of events occuring over a given time interval, the concept of a unit of time has begun to falter, and it is no accident that contemporary mathematical science has put forth the principle of relativity.

To preserve the principle of unity amidst the vortex of changes and the unceasing flood of phenomena, contemporary philosophy in the person of Bergson (whose profoundly Judaic mind is obsessed with the insistent need for practical monotheism) offers us a theory of the system of phenomena. Bergson does not consider phenomena according to the way they submit to the law of temporal succession, but rather according to their spatial extension. He is interested exclusively in the internal connection among phenomena. He liberates this connection from time and considers it independently. Phenomena thus connected to one another form, as it were, a kind of fan whose folds can be opened up in time; however, this fan may also be closed up in a way intelligible to the human mind.

To compare phenomena united in time to form such a fan emphasizes only their internal connection. Thus, instead of the problem of causality (which has for so long dominated the minds of European logicians), [Bergson] poses the problem of the connection alone, purged of any admixture of metaphysics, and therefore more fruitful for scientific discoveries and hypotheses.

A science based on the principle of connection rather than the principle of causality, saves us from the bad infinity of evolutionary theory, not to mention its vulgarized corollary—the theory of progress.

The movement of an endless chain of phenomena having neither beginning nor end is precisely that bad infinity which has nothing to offer the mind seeking unities and connections. Such a concept hypnotizes scientific thought with a simple and easily accessible evolutionism, which, to be sure, gives an appearance of scientific generalization, but only at the cost of renouncing all synthesis and internal structure.

The diffuseness, the non-architectonic character of nineteenth-century European scientific thought at the beginning of the present century has completely demoralized scientific thought. The active mind, which is not just knowledge nor a collection of bits of knowledge, but is rather an instrument, a means of grasping knowledge, has abandoned science, seeing that it can exist independently and find new food wherever it likes. It would be futile to seek such a mind in the scientific life of old Europe. Man's liberated mind has now divorced itself from science. It has turned up everywhere but in science: in poetry, in mysticism, in politics, in theology. As for scientific evolutionism and the theory of progress (insofar as it has not wrung its own neck as modern European science did), it, continuing to operate in the same direction, has beached itself on the shores of theosophy, like an exhuasted swimmer who has reached a joyless shore. Theosophy is the direct heir of the old European philosophy. And its path leads in the same direction: the same bad infinity, the same spinelessness in the doctrine of reincarnation (karma), the same crude and naive materialism in its vulgar conception of the suprasensible world, the same lack of will and taste for the knowledge of activity, as well as a certain kind of omnivorousness based on laziness, an enormous, heavy cud, enough for thousands of stomachs, an interest in everything which verges on indifference, an understanding of everything which verges on an understanding of nothing.

The theory of evolution is particularly dangerous for literature, but the theory of progress is nothing short of suicidal. If one listens to literary historians who defend evolutionism, it would appear that writers think only about how to clear the road for their successors, but never about how to accomplish their own tasks; or it would appear that they are all participants in an inventors' competition for the improvement of some literary machine, although none of them knows the whereabouts of the judges or what purpose the machine serves.

The theory of progress in literature represents the crudest, most repugnant form of schoolboy ignorance. Literary forms change, one set of forms yielding its place to another. However, each change, each gain, is accompanied by a loss, a forfeit. In literature nothing is ever "better," no progress can be made simply because there is no literary machine and no finish line toward which everyone must race as rapidly as possible. This meaningless theory of improvement is not even applicable to the style and form of individual writers, for here as well, each gain is accompanied by a loss or forfeit. Where in *Anna Karenina*, in which Tolstoy assimilated the care for structure and the psychological power of a Flaubertian novel, is the natural instinct and physiological intuition of *War and Peace?* Where in *War and Peace* is the limpid form, the "clarism" of *Childhood and Youth?* The author of *Boris Godunov*, even if he wanted to, could not have repeated his Lyceum verses, just as today no one can write an ode in the manner of Derzhavin. But individual preference is another matter. Just as there are two kinds of geometry, Euclidian and Lobachevskian, so it may be possible to have two kinds of literary history, written in different keys, one treating only the gains, the other only the losses; both, however, would be treating the same subject matter.

Returning to the question of whether Russian literature is a unified whole, and if so, wherein lies its unifying principle, we must immediately eliminate the theory of progress. We shall discuss only the inner connection of the pheonomena involved, and most important, we shall attempt to ascertain the criteria of possible unity, a pivot which will allow us to unfold in time the diverse and scattered phenomena of literature.

Language alone can be acknowledged as the criterion of unity for the literature of a given people, of its conditional unity, all other criteria being conditional, transitory and arbitrary. Although a language is constantly undergoing changes, never freezing in a particular mold even for a moment, moving from one point to another, such points being dazzlingly clear to the mind of the philologist, still, within the confines of its own changes, any given language remains a fixed quantity, a "constant," which is internally unified. Every philologist understands the meaning of personal identity as applied to the self-consciousness of a language. When Latin, once it had spread throughout the Roman lands, blossomed anew and put forth the shoots of the future Romance languages, a new literature was born, juvenile and feeble, perhaps, in comparison with Latin literature, but already a Romance literature.

When the lively and image-laden speech of *The Lay of the Host of Igor* resounded, each turn of phrase temporal, secular, and Russian through and through, Russian literature began. And when Velimir Khlebnikov, the contemporary Russian writer, plunges us into the very thicket of Russian wordroots, into an etymological night, dear to the mind and heart of the intelligent reader, that very same Russian literature, the literature of *The Lay of the Host of Igor,* comes alive once again. The Russian language, just like the Russian national spirit, is formed through ceaseless hybridization, cross-breeding, grafting, and external influences. But it will always remain true to itself in one thing, until our kitchen Latin ceases to resound for us and until pale young shoots of our life begin to sprout on the mighty body of our language, like the Old French song about Saint Eulalia.

Russian is a Hellenistic language. As a result of a number of historical conditions, the vital forces of Hellenic culture, having ceded the West to Latin influences and having tarried for a while in childless Byzantium, rushed headlong into the bosom of Russian speech, imparting to it the self-assured mystery of the Hellenistic world view, the mystery of free incarnation. *That is why Russian became the resonant, speaking flesh it is today.*

If Western cultures and histories lock their language in from the outside, surround it with the walls of State and Church, and become completely permeated by it, so as to decay slowly and blossom again in good season when it disintegrates, Russian culture and history are ever awash on all sides, circumscribed only by the menacing and boundless element of the Russian language, which cannot be contained within any governmental or ecclesiastical form.

The life of the Russian language in Russian historical reality outweighs all other facts in the abundance of its properties, in the abundance of its being. Such abundance appears to all the other phenomena of Russian life as but an inaccessible outer limit. The Hellenistic nature of the Russian language can be identified with its ontological function. The word in its Hellenistic conception is active flesh consummated in the event. Therefore, the Russian language is historical by its very nature, since in its totality it is a turbulent sea of events, a continuous incarnation and activation of rational and breathing flesh. No language resists more strongly than Russian the tendency toward naming and utilitarian application. Russian nominalism, that is, the notion of the reality of the word as such, breathes life into the spirit of our language and connects it with Hellenic philological culture, not etymologically nor literarily, but through the principle of internal freedom, which is equally inherent in both languages.

Utilitarianism in any form is a mortal sin against the Hellenistic nature of the Russian language, regardless of whether it is a tendency towards a telegraphic or stenographic code used for the sake of economy and simple expediency, or whether it is utilitarianism of a higher order, sacrificing language to mystical intuition, anthroposophy, or any kind of omnivorous thought which is ravenous for words.

Andrei Bely, for example, is an unhealthy and negative phenomenon in the life of the Russian language simply because he unsparingly and unceremoniously hounds the word, forcing it to conform to the temperament of his own speculative thought. Choking in his refined prolixity, he cannot sacrifice even one nuance, nor tolerate the slightest break in his capricious thought, and he blows up bridges which he is too lazy to cross. Consequently, after a momentary display of fireworks, he leaves but a pile of broken stones, a melancholy picture of destruction, instead of the abundance of life, organic wholeness, and active equilibrium. The fundamental sin of writers like Andrei Bely is disrespect for the Hellenistic nature of the word, its unsparing exploitation for personal intuitive ends.

The old theme of doubting the capacity of the word to express feelings is reiterated in Russian poetry more than in any other poetry:

> How can the heart fully express itself?
> How can someone else ever know you?

Thus, the language preserves itself from unceremonious attacks.

One cannot measure the growth tempo of a language in terms of the development of life. Attempts to adapt language mechanically to the demands of life are doomed in advance. So-called Futurism, a concept devised by illiterate critics and devoid of all content or scope, is not merely a curiosity of vulgar literary psychology. It assumes an exact meaning if one views it precisely as this forced, mechanical adaptation, this distrust of language, as something which is simultaneously a hare and a tortoise.

Khlebnikov busied himself with words like a mole digging down into the earth to make a path into the future for the entire century, while the representatives of the Moscow metaphorical school, who call themselves Imaginists, exhausted themselves attempting to make language more contemporary. However, they remained far behind language, and it was their fate to be swept aside like so much waste paper.

Chaadaev, in stating his opinion that Russia has no history, that is, that Russia belongs to the unorganized, unhistorical world of cultural phenomena, overlooked one factor — the Russian language. So highly organized, so organic a language is not merely a door into history, but is history itself. For Russia, defection from history, excommunication from the kingdom of historical necessity and continuity, from freedom and teleology, would have been defection from its language. Reduction to a state of "dumbness" for two or three generations could have brought Russia to historical death. Excommunication from language is the equivalent for us to excommunication from history. For that reason, it is certainly true that Russian history travels along the brink, along a ledge, over an abyss, and is on the verge of bursting into nihilism at any moment, that is, of being excommunicated from the word.

Of all contemporary Russian writers, Rozanov felt this danger most acutely. He spent his entire life struggling to preserve the connection with the word, to preserve the philological culture which is so firmly grounded in the Hellenistic nature of Russian speech. An anarchic attitude toward absolutely everything, a total confusion in which anything becomes possible; there is only one thing I cannot do: I cannot live without language, I cannot survive excommunication from the word. Such, approximately, was Rozanov's spiritual state. That anarchistic, nihilistic spirit recognized only one authority: the magic of language, the power of the word, and this, mind you, expressed the attitude not of a poet, nor of a collector or stringer of words, nor was it related to any concern for style; it was but the sentiment of a chatterer or grumbler.

One of Rozanov's books bears the title *By the Cathedral Walls*. It seems to me that Rozanov spent his entire life rummaging about in a soft, yielding void, groping for the walls of Russian culture. Like certain other Russian thinkers, such as Chaadaev, Leontiev, Gershenzon, he could not live without walls, without an acropolis. Everything around him was collapsing, crumbling, everything grew soft and pliable. But we all have the desire to live in history; and in each one of us there is an invincible need to find the solid nut of the Kremlin, the Acropolis: it doesn't matter whether that nucleus is called "state" or "society." Rozanov's craving for the nut and for whatever wall might symbolize that nut completely determined his fate and conclusively exonerated him from all charges of being an unprincipled anarchist.

"It is extremely difficult for one man to be an entire generation — nothing remains but for him to die — it's time for me to perish, for you to flourish." And Rozanov did not live. He died an intelligent and thinking death, as generations die. And Rozanov's life was the death of philology, its withering, the drying up of *belles-lettres* and the desperate battle for life which is warmed by kind words and small talk, by those meanings of words found in parentheses and personal references, but always by philology, only philology.

Rozanov's attitude toward Russian literature was most unliterary. Literature is a social phenomenon, while philology is domestic, intimate. Literature is a lecture, the street; philology is a university seminar, the family. Yes, it is precisely that university seminar where five students, friends calling each other by name and patronymic, listen to their professor, while branches of familiar trees in the university garden climb in through the window. Philology is the family because every family clings to its own intonations, its personal references, and to its own special meanings of words defined in parentheses. The most casual utterance within a family takes on nuances of its own. Moreover, such perpetual, distinctive, and purely philological nuancing defines the atmosphere of family life. Hence, I would derive Rozanov's attraction to the domestic quality of life, which so powerfully defined the entire structure of his literary activity from the philological nature of his soul which, in its indefatigable search for the nut, nibbled and cracked his every word, every utterance, leaving us only empty shells. It comes as no surprise that Rozanov turned out to be an unnecessary and uninfluential writer.

How terrible that man (the eternal philologist) has found a word for this: "death." Is it really possible to name it? Does it even have a name? A name is a definition, "something we already know." So Rozanov defined the essence of his nominalism in a most personal manner: the eternal cognitive movement, the eternal cracking of the nut which comes to nothing because there is no way to gnaw through it. But what kind of literary critic was Rozanov? He only nibbled, he was a casual reader, a lost sheep — neither one thing nor the other...

A critic must know how to devour volumes in search of the essential, and he must generalize. But Rozanov could get bogged down in one line of poetry from any Russian poet, just as he got bogged down in Nekrasov's famous line: "Whether I am driving through the dark street by night..." Rozanov's first comments popped into his head as he was driving along at night in a cab. Another such line can hardly be found in all of Russian poetry.

Rozanov loved the church for expressing the same philological attitude as the family. Here is what he said about it: "The church pronounced such marvelous words over the deceased, words which we are incapable of uttering over our own dead father, son, wife, friend, that is, the church expressed the same intimacy toward, and came as 'near to the soul' of, the dying or dead man as only a mother may experience toward her own dead child. How can one not give up everything for this?..."

The anti-philological spirit against which Rozanov struggled erupted out of the very depths of history; in its own way it was just as inextinguishable a flame as the philological flame.

Such eternal flames exist on the earth and are fed by oil; somewhere, one may accidentally begin to burn and will continue burning for decades. There is no formula which can neutralize it, absolutely nothing can quench it. Luther was a rather poor philologist because instead of argument he offered his inkwell. An anti-philological flame ulcerates the body of Europe ablaze with burning volcanoes on the soil of the West, forever laying waste the ground on which culture erupted. Nothing can neutralize such ravenous flames. They must be allowed to burn, while the accursed places where no one is needed, to which no one will hasten, must be avoided.

Europe devoid of philology is not even America; it is a civilized Sahara desert, cursed by God, an abomination of desolation. As in the past the European Kremlins and Acropolises, the Gothic cities, cathedrals built like forests and onion-domed spherical temples will continue to stand, but people will look upon them without comprehension, and what is more likely, they will take flight, unable to understand what force may have erected them, or what blood may flow in the veins of those powerful architectural monuments surrounding them.

Indeed, what can one say! America is better than this Europe, which, for the moment is still intelligible. Having expended its philological reserves brought over from Europe, America began to act like someone now crazed, now thoughtful; then all of a sudden, she initiated her own particular philology from which Whitman emerged; and he, like the new Adam, began giving things names, began behaving like Homer himself, offering a model for a primitive American poetry of nomenclature. Russia is not America, we have no philological imports; no wild poet like Edgar Allen Poe could sprout up among us like a tree from a palm nut which had crossed the ocean on some ship. The only possible exception is Balmont, the most un-Russian of our poets, a foreign translator of Eolian harps; his kind was never found in the West:

a translator by calling, by birth, even in his most original works.

Balmont's position in Russia is that of a foreign emissary from a non-existent phonetic kingdon, the rare ease of a typical translation without an original. Although Balmont is a Muscovite by birth, an ocean lies between him and Russia. He is a poet completely alien to Russian poetry; he leaves less of a trace on it than his translations of Shelley or Poe, even though his own verse forces one to believe in the existence of highly interesting originals.

We have no Acropolis. Even today out culture is still wandering and not finding its walls. Nevertheless, each word in Dal's dictionary is a kernel of the Acropolis, a small Kremlin, a winged fortress of nominalism, rigged out in the Hellenic spirit for the relentless battle against the formless element, against non-existence, which threatens our history from every side.

In the same way that Rozanov represents the domestic Hellenism of God's fools and the poor in Russian literature, Annensky represents heroic Hellenism, martial philology. Annensky's lyric poetry and his tragedies can be compared to the wooden fortifications, the walled towns far out in the steppes, which served to defend local princes against the Pechenegs, against the night of the Khazars.

> No longer do I begrudge my dark fate:
> Even Ovid was once naked and impotent.

Annensky's inability to wield any influence, to serve either as mediator or translator, is truly astonishing. In a most original manner, he grasped in his talons all that was foreign, and still soaring high in the sky arrogantly dropped his plunder, allowing it to fall as it would. And the eagle of his poetry which had seized as its prey Euripides, Mallarmé, Leconte de Lisle, brought us nothing but handfuls of dry grass:

> Listen, a madman knocks at your door,
> God knows where and with whom he spent the night,

His eyes wander, his speech is wild,
And his hand is full of pebbles.
Take heed, he is emptying the other,
Scattering dry leaves over you.

Gumilev called Annensky a great European poet. Is seems to
me that when Europeans recognize him (having meekly educated
their children in the Russian language as in the past they educated
them in the ancient languages and classical poetry), they will be
frightened by the audacity of this regal bird of prey who abducted
the dove Eurydice from them for the Russian snows, who tore
the classical shawl from Phaedra's shoulders, and who, as befits a
Russian poet, tenderly placed an animal's pelt over Ovid's still
frozen body. How astonishing is Annensky's fate! Having touched
the treasures of the world, he preserved only a piteous handful
for himself, or rather raised a handful of dust and tossed it back
into the flaming treasure house of the West. When Annensky kept
vigil, everyone was sleeping. The realists snored. *The Scales* had
not yet been founded. The young student Vyacheslav Ivanovich
Ivanov was studying with Mommsen and writing a monograph in
Latin about Roman taxation. At the same time, the director of
the Gymnasium at Tsarskoe Selo was struggling late into the night
with Euripides, imbibing the snake poison of wise Hellenic
speech, preparing an infusion of bitter, absinth-flavored verse of a
kind no one before or after him could write. Moreover, for Annensky poetry was a domestic affair, as Euripides was a domestic
writer, filled with personal references and words whose special
meanings were found only in parentheses. Annensky perceived all
of world poetry as a shaft of light sent forth by Hellas. He understood distance; he experienced both its ardor and its chill, and he
never attempted superficial combinations of Russian and Hellenic
worlds. The lesson to be drawn from Annensky's creative work
for Russian poetry is not concerned with Hellenization *per se*,
but rather involves internal Hellenism, domestic Hellenism as it
were, that which is suitable to the spirit of the Russian language.
Hellenism is an earthenware pot, oven tongs, a milk jug, kitchen

44

utensils, dishes; it is anything which surrounds the body. Hellenism is the warmth of the hearth experienced as something sacred; it is anything which imparts some of the external world to man, just as the pelts placed over the old man's shoulders in the following lines express a similar sense of awe:

When the rapid river froze
And the winter winds raged,
With fluffy pelts they covered
The old man's saintly frame.

Hellenism is the conscious surrounding of man with domestic utensils, and the humanizing and warming of the surrounding world with the most delicate teleological warmth. Hellenism is any kind of stove near which a man sits, treasuring its heat as something akin to his own internal body heat. And finally, Hellenism is the Egyptian funerary ship in which the dead are carried, into which everything required for the continuation of man's earthly wanderings is put, down to perfume phials, mirrors, and combs. Hellenism is a system in the Bergsonian sense of the term which man unfolds around himself like a fan of phenomena freed of their temporal dependence, phenomena subjected by the human "I" to an internal connection.

In the Hellenistic sense, symbols are domestic utensils, but then any object brought into man's sacred circle could become a utensil and consequently, a symbol. One may rightfully ask then if an exclusive, specially contrived symbolism is necessary for Russian poetry? Is not such contrived symbolism a sin against the Hellenistic nature of our language, which creates images like domestic utensils for man's use?

There is essentially no difference between the word and the image. The word is merely an image which has been sealed up, which cannot be touched. An image is inappropriate for everyday use, just as an icon lamp would be inappropriate for lighting a cigarette. But such sealed-up images are also very necessary. Man loves interdictions, and even an uncivilized man will put magic

prohibitions, "taboos," on certain objects. Nevertheless, once removed from circulation, the sealed-up image is inimical to man,
for in its own way it becomes a kind of scarecrow, or effigy.

Anything transient is but a likeness. Let's take for example
a rose and the sun, a dove and a girl. To the Symbolists, not one
of these images is interesting in itself: the rose is a likeness of the
sun, the sun is a likeness of a rose, a dove — of a girl, and a girl —
of a dove. Images are gutted like scarecrows and packed with foreign content. In place of the Symbolist forest, we are left with a
workshop producing scarecrows.

This is where professional Symbolism leads. Perception is
demoralized. Nothing is real, genuine. Nothing is left but a terrifying quadrille of "correspondences" nodding to one another. Eternal winking. Never a clear word, nothing but hints and reticent
whispers. The rose nods to the girl, the girl to the rose. No one
wants to be himself.

That remarkable epoch in the development of Russian poetry known as Symbolism (defined by the group associated with
the journal *The Scales*) which, although standing on clay feet, developed in the course of two decades into a colossal structure, is
best defined as the epoch of pseudo-Symbolism. However, do not
take this definition to refer to Classicism; such a reference would
degrade its magnificent poetry and the fertile style of Racine.
Pseudo-Classicism was a slogan adopted out of schoolboy ignorance and applied to a great style. Russian pseudo-Symbolism is
truly pseudo-Symbolism. Jourdain discovered in his old age that
he had been speaking "prose" all his life. The Russian Symbolists
discovered the same prose, the primordial, image-bearing nature
of the word. They sealed up all words, all images, designating
them exclusively for liturgical use. An extremely awkward situation resulted: no one could move, nor stand up, nor sit down.
One could no longer eat at a table because it was no longer simply
a table. One could no longer light a lamp because it might signify
unhappiness later.

A man was no longer master in his own house. He had to live
either in a church or in a sacred grove of the Druids; a man could

46

not rest his eyes for there was no place for him to seek peace. The domestic utensils all rose in rebellion. The broom begged for the Sabbath; the kettle refused to boil and demanded an absolute significance for itself (as if boiling had no absolute significance). The master was chased out of his house and no longer dared to enter. What can be done when a word is fettered to its meaning: doesn't this amount to serfdom? But the word is not a thing. Its significance is not a translation of itself. Indeed, it has never happened that anyone has christened a thing, calling it by an invented name. The most appropriate and, in scientific terms, the most correct approach, is to regard the word as an image, that is, as a verbal representation. In this way, the question of form and content is avoided, phonetics being the form, all the rest — content. Also avoided is the question of giving primary significance to the word as opposed to its phonetic nature. The verbal representation is a complex composite of phenomena, it is a connection, a "system." The significance of the word may be viewed as a candle burning inside a paper lantern, and conversely, its phonetic value, the so-called phoneme, may be located inside the significance, just as that candle may be inside that lantern.

The old psychology knew only how to objectify the representation, and, having overcome this naive solipsism, regarded representations as something external. According to that view, the decisive factor was that of givenness. The givenness of the products of our consciousness makes them like the objects of the external world, thus permitting us to regard representations as something objective. However, the extremely rapid humanization of science, including the theory of knowledge, forces us to move in another direction. We can consider representations not only as objective data of consciousness, but also as human organs, just like the liver or the heart.

In its application to the word, such an interpretation of verbal representations opens up broad new perspectives, allowing us to dream about the creation of an organic poetics, a poetics of a biological rather than legislative nature, a poetics which would destroy the canon in the name of the internal unity of the organ-

47

ism, a poetics which would exhibit all the traits of biological science.

The organic school of Russian poetry which developed as a result of the creative initiative of Gumilev and Gorodetsky early in 1912, and which Akhmatova, Narbut, Zenkevich and the author of these lines officially joined, took upon itself the task of constructing just such a poetics. The small amount of literature on Acmeism plus the frugal attitude toward theory exhibited by its leaders makes it study difficult. Acmeism arose out of a sense of repulsion: "Down with Symbolism! Long live the living rose!" — such was its original slogan.

In his day Gorodetsky attempted to inoculate Acmeism with his literary world view, "Adamism," a form of the doctrine of the new earth and the new Adam. His efforts were unsuccessful; Acmeism was not concerned with world views, but brought with it a host of new sensations of taste, much more valuable than ideas; of these, the most significant was the taste for the integral verbal representation, the image, understood in a new organic way. Literary schools thrive on tastes rather than ideas. To express a number of new ideas while ignoring new tastes means to establish a new poetics, not a new school. On the other hand, a school can be founded on tastes alone, without any new ideas. Acmeist tastes rather than Acmeist ideas dealt Symbolism its fatal blow. For Acmeist ideas turned out, at least in part, to be borrowed from the Symbolists, and Vyacheslav Ivanov himself was a great help in the formulation of Acmeist theory. But see what a miracle occurred: new blood began to course through the veins of those who live within Russian poetry. It has been said that faith will move mountains. Because a new taste arose in Russia at the beginning of the century, such massifs as Rabelais, Shakespeare, and Racine were removed from their bases and came to pay us a visit. The moving force of Acmeism in the sense of its active love of literature — the difficulties and burdens of literature — is extraordinary, and the key to this active love was precisely this change in taste, the indomitable will to create a man-centered poetry and poetics, with man as master of his own home, not man flattened into a wafer by the horrors of pseudo-Symbolism; genuine Symbolism surrounded by symbols, that is, by domestic utensils having their own verbal representations, just as they have their own vital organs.

More than once in Russian society there have been periods when the moving spirit of Western literature was read with genius. Thus did Pushkin and his entire generation read Chénier. Thus did the following generation, the generation of Odoevsky, read Schelling, E.T.A. Hoffmann, and Novalis. Thus did the men of the 1860's read their Buckle, although nothing significant emerged on either side, and in that it was even impossible to locate the ideal reader. The wind of Acmeism turned the pages of the Classicists and the Romantics, opening them to just that page which most appealed to the age. Racine was opened to *Phèdre*, Hoffmann to *The Serapion Brothers*. Chénier's *Iambes* were discovered along with Homer's *Iliad*.

Furthermore, Acmeism is a social as well as a literary manifestation in Russian history. With Acmeism a moral force was reborn in Russian poetry. Bryusov said:

> I want my free boat to sail in every direction;
> And I shall praise the Lord and the Devil equally.

This bankrupt "nihilism" will never be repeated in Russian poetry. Until now the social inspiration of Russian poetry has reached no further than the idea of "citizen," but there is a loftier principle than "citizen," there is the concept of "Man."

As opposed to the civic poetry of the past, modern Russian poetry must educate not merely citizens, but "Men." The ideal of perfect manliness is provided by the style and practical demands of our age. Everything has become heavier and more massive, thus man must become harder, for he must be the hardest thing on earth; he must be to the earth what the diamond is to glass. The hieratic, that is to say, the sacred character of poetry arises out of the conviction that man is harder than everything else in the world.

The age will shout itself out, culture will fall asleep, and the people will be reborn, having given their utmost to the new social class, and this current will draw the fragile ship of the human word away with it, out into the open sea of the future where there is no sympathetic understanding, where cheerless commentary will replace the fresh wind of contemporary enmity and sympathy. How can one equip this ship for its distant voyage, without furnishing it with all the necessities for so foreign and cherished a reader? Once more I shall liken a poem to an Egyptian funerary ship. In that ship everything is provided for life, nothing is forgotten. But I can already see in this original formulation innumerable potential objections and the beginning of a reaction against Acmeism equal to the crisis of pseudo-Symbolism. Pure biology is inappropriate to the construction of a poetics. A biological analogy may be good and fruitful, but to apply it consistently would be to develop a biological canon, no less oppressive and intolerable than the canon of pseudo-Symbolism. "The rational abyss of the Gothic soul" gapes forth from the physiological conception of art. Salieri deserves respect and fervent love. It was not his fault that he heard the music of algebra as vibrantly as living harmony.

Instead of the romantic, the idealist, or the aristocrat dreaming about the pure symbols, about the abstract esthetics of the word, instead of Symbolism, Futurism and Imaginism, there has arisen a living poetry of the object-word; its creator is not Mozart, the idealist dreamer, but Salieri, the stern and strict craftsman, extending a hand to the master craftsman of things and material values, to the builder and creator of the world of things.

Translated by Jane Gary Harris

Osip Mandelstam

ON THE ADDRESSEE

I would like to know what it is about a madman which creates that most terrifying impression of madness. It must be his dilated pupils, because they are blank and stare at you so absently, focusing on nothing in particular. It must be his mad speech, because in speaking to you the madman never takes you into account, nor even recognizes your existence as if wishing to ignore your presence, to show absolutely no interest in you. What we fear most in a madman is that absolute and terrifying indifference which he displays toward us. Nothing strikes terror in a man more than another man who shows no concern for him whatsoever. Cultural pretense, the politeness by which we constantly affirm our interest in one another, thus contains a profound meaning for us all.

Normally, when a man has something to say, he goes to people, he seeks out an audience. A poet does just the opposite: he runs "to the shores of desert waves, to broad and resonant oaks." His abnormality is obvious... Suspicion of madness descends upon the poet. And people are right when they call a man mad whose speech is addressed to inanimate objects, to nature, but never to his living brethren. And they would be within their rights to stand back terrified of the poet, as of a madman, if, indeed, his words were actually addressed to no one. However, such is not the case.

The view of the poet as "God's bird" is very dangerous and fundamentally false. There is no reason to believe that Pushkin had the poet in mind when he composed his song about the bird. But even insofar as Pushkin's bird is concerned, the matter is not all that simple. Before he commences singing, the bird "hearkens the voice of God." Obviously, the one who orders

52

the bird to sing, listens to its song. The bird "flaps its wings and sings," because a "natural harmony" unites the bird with God, an honor even the greatest poetic genius does not dare to dream of... Then to whom does the poet speak? This is a question which still plagues us, which is still extremely pertinent, because the Symbolists always avoided it, and never formulated it succinctly. By ignoring the concomitant juridical, so to speak, relationship which attends the act of speaking (for example: I am speaking: this means people are listening to me and listening to me for a reason, not out of politeness, but because they are committed to hear me out), Symbolism turned its attention exclusively to acoustics. It relinquished sound to the architecture of the spirit, but with its characteristic egoism, followed its meanderings under the arches of an alien psyche. Symbolism calculated the increase in fidelity produced by fine acoustics, and called it magic. In this respect, Symbolism brings to mind the French medieval proverb about "Prêtre Martin," who simultaneously performed and attended mass. The Symbolist poet is not only a musician, he is Stradivarius himself, the great violin-maker, fastidiously calculating the proportions of the "sound-box," the psyche of the audience. Depending on these proportions, a stroke of the bow may produce a sound truly splendid in its richness or an impoverished and unsure sound. But, my friends, a musical piece has its own independent existence regardless of the performer, the concert hall, or the violin. Why then should the poet be so prudent and solicitous? And more significant, where is that supplier of poet's needs, the supplier of living violins—the audience whose psyche is equivalent to the "shell" of Stradivarius' products? We do not know, nor will we ever know, where this audience is... François Villon wrote for the Parisian mob of the mid-fifteenth century, but the charm of his poetry lives on today...

Every man has his friends. Why shouldn't the poet turn to his friends, turn to those who are naturally close to him? At the critical moment, the seafarer tosses into the ocean waves a bottle containing a message: his name and the details of his fate. Wandering along the dunes many years later, I happen upon it in the sand. I read the message, recognize the date of the event, the last will and testament of someone who has passed on. I have the right to do so. I haven't opened someone else's mail. The message in the bottle was addressed to its finder. I found it. Hence, I have become its secret addressee.

> My gift is poor, my voice is not loud,
> But I am alive. And on this earth
> My presence is a friend to someone:
> My distant heir shall find it
> In my verse; how do I know? my soul
> And his soul shall find a common ground,
> As I have found a friend in my generation,
> I will find a reader in posterity.

Reading this poem of Baratynsky, I experience the same feeling I would if such a bottle came into my possession. The ocean, in all the enormity of its element, came to its aid, helped it to fulfill its destiny. And that feeling of providence overwhelms the finder. Two equally lucid facts emerge from the tossing of the seafarer's bottle to the waves and from the dispatching of Baratynsky's poem. The message, just like the poem, was addressed to no one in particular. And yet both have addresses: the message is addressed to the person who happened across the bottle in the sand; the poem is addressed to "the reader in posterity." I would like to know who, among the readers of Baratynsky's poem, did not feel that joyous and awesome excitement experienced when someone is unexpectedly hailed by name.

Balmont asserted:

> I know no wisdom suitable for others,
> Moments only do I enclose in my verse.
> In each fleeting moment I see worlds
> Brimming with inconstant, iridescent games.

Don't curse, wisemen, what am I to you?
I'm but a cloud brimming o'er with flame,
I'm but a cloud, and I shall float on
And hail all dreamers. But you I shall not hail.

What a contrast between the unpleasant, ingratiating tone of these lines and the profound and modest dignity of Baratysnky's verse! Balmont seeks to vindicate himself, as if he were offering an apology. Unforgivable! Intolerable for a poet! The only thing which is impossible to forgive. After all, isn't poetry the consciousness of being right? Balmont expresses no such consciousness here. He has clearly lost his bearings. His opening line murders the entire poem. From the very outset the poet declares definitively that we hold no interest for him:

I know no wisdom suitable for others.

He does not suspect that we may pay him back in kind: if we hold no interest for you, you hold no interest for us. What do I care about his cloud when there are so many floating about... At least genuine clouds don't scorn people. Balmont's rejection of the "addressee" is like a red line drawn through all his poetry, severely depreciating its value. In his verse, Balmont is constantly treating someone with disrespect, brusquely, superciliously. This "someone" is the secret addressee of whom we have been talking. Unperceived and unrecognized by Balmont, he cruelly avenges him. When we converse with someone, we search his face for sanctions, for a confirmation of our sense of rightness. Even more so the poet. But the poet's invaluable consciousness of being right is frequently missing from Balmont's poetry because he lacks a constant addressee. Hence, those two unpleasant, yet antithetical, traits in Balmont's poetry: sycophancy and insolence. Balmont's insolence is artifical, contrived. His drive to vindicate himself is downright sick. He is incapable of uttering the word "I" softly. He must shout "I":

I am a sudden outburst
I am a thunderclap breaking.

On the scales of Balmont's poetry, the pan containing the "I"
dips decisively and unjustly below the "Not-I." The latter is far
too light. Balmont's blatant individualism is very unpleasant. As
opposed to the calm solipsism of Sologub, which never insults
anyone, Balmont's individualism emerges at the expense of
an alien "I." Note how Balmont enjoys stunning his readers
by turning abruptly to the intimate form of address. In this he
resembles a nasty, evil hypnotist. Balmont's intimate "thou"
never reaches the addressee, for it shoots past its mark like an
arrow released from a bow pulled too taut.

As I have found a friend in my generation
I will find a reader in posterity...

Baratynsky's piercing eye darts beyond generations (but in
each generation there are friends) to halt in front of an as yet unknown, but well-defined "reader." Thus, each person who comes
to know Baratynsky's poetry feels himself to be that "reader," to
be that chosen one, the one who is hailed by name... Why then
should there not be a concrete, living addressee, a "representative
of the age," a "friend in this generation"? I will answer that: because appealing to a concrete addressee dismembers poetry, removes its wings, deprives it of air, of the freedom of flight. The
fresh air of poetry is the element of surprise. In addressing a
known quantity, we can speak only of what is already known.
This is an absolute, inflexible psychological law. Its significance
for poetry cannot be underestimated.

The fear of facing a concrete addressee, of facing an audience of our "age," or that "friend in this generation," has doggedly pursued poets of all ages. And the greater the poet's genius,
the more severely he has suffered from this fear. Hence, the notorious hostility between the artist and society. What may be
meaningful to the prose writer or essayist, the poet finds absolutely meaningless. The difference between prose and poetry may

be defined as follows. The prose writer always addresses himself to a concrete audience, to the dynamic representatives of his age. Even when making prophecies, he bears his future contemporaries in mind. His subject matter brims over into the present, in keeping with the physical law of unequal levels. Consequently, the prose writer is compelled to stand "higher" than, to be "superior" to, society. Since instruction is the nerve of prose, the prose writer requires a pedestal. Poetry, however, is quite another matter. The poet is bound only to a providential contemporary. He is not compelled to tower over his age, to appear superior to his society. Indeed, François Villon stood far below the median moral and intellectual levels of the culture of the fifteenth century.

Pushkin's quarrel with the common people, with the "mob," may be viewed as an example of that hostility between the poet and a concrete audience which I am trying to elucidate. Pushkin, with incredible impartiality, appealed to the mob to try to justify itself. And, as it turned out, the mob was not so wild and unenlightened. But then how did this very considerate "mob," imbued with the best intentions, wrong the poet? In the process of vindicating itself, one tactless phrase slipped from its tongue, overflowed the poet's cup of patience and kindled his enmity:

Here we are, all ears.

What a tactless phrase! The stupid vulgarity of these seemingly harmless words is obvious. Not without reason did the poet indignantly interrupt the mob right at this juncture... The sight of a hand begging for alms is repulsive, but the sight of ears pricked up, ready to listen, may provide a source of inspiration to anyone, an orator, a politician, a prose writer, to anyone, that is, except a poet... Concrete people, the "philistines of poetry," those who comprise the mob, will permit anyone "to offer them bold lessons." They are generally prepared to listen to anyone, but if he is a poet, he must designate a proper address: "to such and such a mob." So it is that simple people, like children, feel flattered when they can read their names on the envelope of a letter. And there have been entire epochs when the charm and essence of poetry were sacrificed to this far from inoffensive demand. Such verse included the pseudo-civic poetry and the tedious lyrics of the 1880s. Nevertheless, the civic and the tendentious may contain a beauty of its own, for example:

> A great poet, perhaps, you'll never be,
> But to be a citizen is your obligation—

These lines are remarkable, flapping their powerful wings, flying toward a providential addressee. But if that addressee were a once famous Russian philistine of a particular decade, familiar to us all, the lines would simply bore us.

Yes, when I address someone, I do not know whom I am addressing; furthermore, I do not care to know, nor can I want to know, him. Without dialogue, lyric poetry cannot exist. But there is only one thing that pushes us into the addressee's embrace: the desire to be astonished by our own words, to be enchanted by their originality and unexpectedness. Logic is pitiless. Thus, if I know the person I am addressing, I know in advance how he will react to my words, whatever I say, and consequently, I will not succeed in being astonished in his astonishment, in rejoicing in his joy, in loving in his love. The distance of separation blots out the features of the loved one. Only from a distance do I feel the desire to tell him something important, something I could not utter seeing his face before me as a known quantity. Allow me to formulate this observation more succinctly: our taste for communication is in inverse proportion to our real knowledge of the addressee and in direct proportion to our active attempt to interest him in himself. Acoustics can take care of itself, hence we need not be concerned about it. Distance, however, is another matter. Whispering to a neighbor is boring. But it is downright maddening to bore one's own soul (Nadson). On the other hand, exchanging signals with the planet Mars (not merely in the realm of fantasy) is a task worthy of a lyric poet. Here we come upon Fyodor Sologub in the flesh. In many ways, Sologub is a most interesting antipode to Balmont. Certain qualities missing in Balmont's work abound in Sologub's poetry. For instance, love and admiration of the addressee, and the poet's consciousness of being right. These two remarkable characteristics of Sologub's poetry are closely related to that "enormous distance" which he presumes lies between himself and his ideal "friend"-addressee:

> My mysterious friend, my distant friend,
> Behold.
> I am the cold and mournful
> Light at dawn...
> And so cold and mournful
> In the morning,
> My mysterious friend, my distant friend,
> I shall die.

In order that these lines reach their destination, perhaps hundreds of years are necessary, as many as a planet needs to send its light to another planet. Consequently, Sologub's lines continue to live long after they were written, as an event, not merely as a sign of an experience which has passed.

And so, although separate poems (in the form of epistles, or dedications) may be addressed to concrete persons, poetry as a whole is always addressed to a more or less distant, unknown addressee, but in whose existence the poet does not doubt, not doubting in himself. Metaphysics has nothing to do with this. Only reality can bring to life a new reality. The poet is no homunculus, and there is absolutely no basis for ascribing to him characteristics of spontaneous generation.

The point is very simply this: if we had no friends, we would not write letters to them, and we would not gain satisfaction from the psychological freshness and novelty peculiar to this occupation.

Translated by Jane Gary Harris

Vladislav Khodasevich

THE SHAKEN TRIPOD

In every artistic work we find a series of goals that the author sets for himself. These goals can belong to varying orders: philosophical, psychological, descriptive, and so on—even up to and including purely formal ones. These goals are stated with varying degrees of consciousness. Often in the creative process one such problem is solved more fully than the others, which appear suppressed, muted, playing only a subordinate role. But the very presence of a series of problems in a work of art is unavoidable; in particular, the poet, by the very nature of his craft, cannot set less than two problems for himself, for poetry itself contains at least two forms of content: the logical and the aural.

One of the most amazing characteristics of Pushkin's poetry and, perhaps, one of the secrets of its well-known harmoniousness, lies in an unusual balance with which the poet resolves the two parallel problems. The evenness with which he divides his attention between them, and the exhaustive fullness with which he resolves them simultaneously, are amazing. In a piece the purport of which is the blessings of a peaceful, domestic, laboring life, one finds depicted with equal attention the kind house spirits, to whom the poem is addressed, the prayerful humility of the inhabitant of the house, and finally, the manor itself, with its forest, garden, time-worn fence, noisy maples and green slop of hills. The goals of a lyricist, who transmits his own spontaneous feeling, and those of a folklorist or a painter, are resolved each separately, with complete fullness. At the same time and with equal force, three different feelings are evoked in the reader. The three planes of the picture lend it a stereoscopic depth.

Such series of parallel goals can be discovered in any of Pushkin's works, but nowhere does his mastery in solving his problems attain such heights as in the long narrative poems. Here one is amazed not only by the mastery in resolving the problems, but also by their quantity. One can draw up a long list of themes which receive a full and deep elaboration, for example, in *The Bronze Horseman*. First of all, it is a national tragedy in the narrow definition of the word: here is depicted, as has often been pointed out, the collision of Petrine autocracy with the inherent love of freedom in the masses. This tragedy acquires a special significance if one looks at the rebellion of poor Evgeny as a protest of the personality against coercion by the state, as a collision of private and common interests. This tragedy will receive a special shade of meaning if one would remember that it is indeed Pushkin's Peter that sees Petersburg as a window to Europe. Here will be lanced a part of that most damned question, the name of which is: Europe and us. But it is not to be forgotten that *The Bronze Horseman* is at the same time an answer to the Polish events of 1831, that the rebellion of Evgeny against Peter is the mutiny of Poland against Russia. Finally, as I already had occasion to point out, *The Bronze Horseman* is one of the links in the chain of Pushkin's Petersburg tales, which depict the collision of man with demons. However, the aims of this long poem are far from being exhausted by what has already been said. He who will see in it a guileless tale of the broken hopes of love of an insignificant man will be correct, as would be he who would single out from the poem its descriptive side and underscore in it the marvelous description of Petersburg, prosperous at first, then "surfacing like the Triton" from the waves of the flood, which in itself is described with documentary precision. Finally, we would be incorrect if we were not to give the *Introduction* to the poem its due, as an example of sparkling polemic against Mickiewicz.

But parallel goals in Pushkin are a theme for a major investigation. Here I touched upon it only for the purpose of reminding us, by means of a concrete example, how a series of problems set forth by the poet lends his works series of parallel meanings. Pushkin shows the object from a whole multitude of points of view. To the objects of his imagined world he lends the same fullness of existence, the same relief, the same multidimensional and polychromatic qualities which are possessed by objects in the real world. For this reason to each of his works one can apply a whole series of criteria that are also applicable to objects which surround us. Just as the artist, the geometrician, the botanist, and the physicist reveal in one and the same object different sets of qualities, so too in the works of Pushkin different people with equal reason find different things. Pushkin is indeed a *creator,* for the life created by his thought is full and diversified. There is something miraculous in the genesis of this life. But there is nothing miraculous, or even surprising, in the fact that, having once appeared, the world created by Pushkin finds a fate of its own, its own independently flowing history.

The exceptional multiplicity of themes in Pushkin brings an equally exceptional multiplicity of meanings to his works. And if the works of all great artists, encompassing in themselves whole series of meanings, call forth a corresponding series of interpretations, then the works of Pushkin belong to some of the most tempting in this respect. This temptation flows out of the very nature of Pushkin's realism. If we also take into account the natural quality of criticism to reflect the fate of the critic at least to the same degree as that of the poet, in other words, if we recall with what inevitability the works of great artists acquire differing hues, meanings, and significance in the eyes of changing generations and peoples, all the diversity of meanings that are found in the works of Pushkin will then become historically understandable. Pushkin has been and is interpreted in varying ways. But the multiplicity of interpretations is, so to speak, the professional risk of geniuses—and one must confess that in recent times the unexpectedness of opinions expressed about Pushkin becomes particularly striking. True, much of what is said is correct and perceptive, but many things astound one by their distance from the spontaneous and unbiased impression that one receives from the works of the poet. And finally, much goes directly against the grain of the incontestable clarity of Pushkin's text. I do not by any means have in mind the conscious distortions and the juggling done for the sake of literary and, often, worldly gain, though, to our misfortune and shame this also happens. But such occurrences are accidental, and say nothing of this internal correlation between Pushkin and our age. On the other hand, very representative are some impeccably conscientious works in which interpretations are given which find too hazy a corroboration in Pushkin's text. Generalizations are made which are too bold, hypotheses which have very little probability are expressed. With all sorts of reservations, I would nevertheless cite as one of the examples Gershenzon's book *The Wisdom of Pushkin,* which is extremely valuable and interesting, both in the originality and the profundity of many thoughts. There is much truth said in it about Pushkin—but nonetheless Gershenzon, an historian of literature acting the role of Pushkin's interpreter, proved to be a man of a different inner makeup than was Pushkin himself: Gershenzon already stands on that invisible line by means of which history separates epochs.

And Gershenzon is not alone. With each new day more such critics of greater or lesser stature appear and will continue to appear. If, as I have already said, the face of a great writer unavoidably changes in the eyes of changing generations, then in our days, and, furthermore, in reference to the endlessly polymorphous Pushkin, this change will come about with exceptional force. Our history has made such a leap that between yesterday and today there has appeared a void of some sort, which is psychologically painful as an open wound. And everything around us has changed: not only the political system and all social interrelations, but also the outer forms, the very rhythm, system, daily aspects, and style of life. We have new customs, mores, clothes, even, if you like, fashions. The Petersburg in which we shall go home tonight is not the Petersburg of the not-so-long-ago. The world which surrounds us has become a different one. The changes which have occurred are deep and stable. They had already begun to manifest themselves since 1905. 1917 was only the last jolt which to our eyes showed that we are present at the change of two epochs. The former Russia, and with that the Russia of Pushkin, immediately and suddenly moved away from us to an immeasurably greater distance than it would have in the same period during an evolutionary course of events. The Petrine and Petersburg period of Russian history has ended. Whatever lies ahead, the old will not return. A return is unthinkable, be it historically or psychologically.

And thus, in application to Pushkin's legacy, one must draw certain conclusions from the conditions which have arisen. It is not only that Pushkin's works will undergo a series of changes in the consciousness of the readers. I have already spoken of these changes as distinct evidence of the fact that Pushkin is already, so to speak, detached from his own time and has entered the open sea of history, where it is his fate, like that of Sophocles or Dante, to be covered with a growth of interpretations and commentaries. But something else will also happen.

In the history of Russian literature there already was a moment when Pisarev "abolished" Pushkin, declaring him superfluous and insignificant. But the mainstream of Pisarev's views did not draw a wide following of readers and soon disappeared. From that time on, the name of Pisarev was more than once pronounced with a feeling of annoyance, even anger, which was natural for connoisseurs of literature, but impossible for an historian, who hearkens with indifference to good and evil. The Pisarev attitude toward Pushkin was unwise and tasteless. But nevertheless, it was augured by the ideas which were then in the air; to a certain degree it expressed the spirit of the times, and by putting it into words Pisarev expressed the viewpoint of a certain part of Russian society. Those on whom Pisarev leaned were people of a limited mind and squalid aesthetic development—but it is in no way possible to say that they were bad people, hooligans, or obscurantists. In the primordial schism of Russian society they stood, in fact, on the side not with the worse half, but with the better half.

This was the first eclipse of Pushkin's sun. It seems to me that the second one is not far away. It will not be expressed in such a coarse form. Pushkin will be neither mocked nor insulted.

But a cooling-off toward him lies ahead.

Of course, one cannot point at the precise minute on the clock when this second eclipse will become evident to all. Also one cannot among people define those circles, those groups of people, on whom his shadow is cast. But already these people who do not see Pushkin are interspersed in our midst. Already many do not hear Pushkin as we hear him, because from the roar of the last six years their ears have become a bit deaf. They are forced to translate Pushkin into the language of their own sensations, which are dulled by the heart-rending dramas of the cinema. Already many of Pushkin's images say less to them than they say to us, for they do not see clearly the world from which these images are drawn, in contact to which these images were born. And here again these people are not renegades, not degenerates: they are simply new people. Many of them, still youths without hair on the upper lip, almost boys, were sent out into the trenches, saw whole mountains of corpses, themselves tore apart many human bellies, burned many cities, destroyed many roads, trampled out many fields, and then returned yesterday, spreading their mental contagion. It is not their fault—but nonetheless they still have a lot of growing up to do in order to attain the understanding of Pushkin. Meanwhile, they do not fully recognize the necessity to educate oneself and to grow spiritually—though in other spheres of life, especially in the practical, they show a great deal of activity.

And it is not only among readers: among Russian poets one can discover much the same thing. Much in Pushkin is almost incomprehensible to some of the younger poets, for the reason, by the way, that they are not always familiar enough with all that surrounds Pushkin; because the spirit and the style of his epoch are alien to them, and they have not come into contact with any remnants of his era. The same thing should be said of the language. Perhaps they even follow Pushkin's exhortation to learn the language from Moscow's women bakers of liturgical breads—but they themselves no longer speak the same language. Many shades of Pushkin's lexicon, so meaningful to us, to them are no more than archaisms. Some words with which a most valuable tradition is connected and which you introduce into your own poetry with great care, not knowing whether you have an inner right to use them—to such a degree they have an exceptional sacramental meaning for us—prove to be simply pale in the judgment of the young poet—who does not even suspect what other things these words might mean to you, other than what they mean for everyone according to Dahl's dictionary. Occasionally whole series of the most cherished intimate thoughts and feelings prove to be inexpressible by means other than those found within the bounds of Pushkin's lexicon and syntax—and this, the most cherished, is seen only as "stylization."

One cannot help pointing at the same time to the recent resurgence of the tendency to sever form from content, and to the propagation of the idea of the primacy of form—much the way the primacy of content was preached during the first eclipse of Pushkin. Both the latter and the former are equally inimical to the whole spirit of Pushkin's poetry. Those who state that Pushkin is great by virtue of the virtuosity of his form, and that therefore his content is a secondary thing, because content in poetry has no meaning, are really "Pisarevites" in reverse. Not knowing this themselves, they are slanderers and secret enemies of Pushkin, acting in the guise of friends.

In saying all this I do not at all have in mind the Futurists, but rather the representatives of the more "moderate" literary groups. One could recount a large number of sad and curious anecdotes which prove that a direct elementary misunderstanding and ignorance of Pushkin is a phenomenon that is equally prevalent in young literary circles and among readers. All of this is the result of a growing inattentiveness to Pushkin. It arises from the fact that Pushkin's epoch is no longer our epoch, but he has not yet become a writer of antiquity, so that a scholarly study of Pushkin, whatever huge steps it may have taken, is still the legacy of a few. The importance and value of such study are not yet understood by either the mass reader or the mass writer. And thus the naive youth of our day, equally the reader and the young poet, decide that Pushkin is simply "old-fashioned."

The very fact that the cooling-off toward Pushkin is developed not in the flasks of the literary laboratory, that it is equally common to the reader and the writer, indicates that it feeds on the quotidian circumstances of reality. As in the days of Pisarev, the cooling-off toward Pushkin, the forgetting of Pushkin and insensitivity to him is supported by the mass of readers, that is, it arises for reasons that are, in the literary-social sense, organic. The reasons are not the same ones today that they were in the days of Pisarev, the aloofness from Pushkin now is motivated by other considerations, but it may prove to be more durable, spread wider, and last for a longer period of time, because it is prepared by historical circumstances of vast import and scope.

The Revolution brought much that is good. But we all know that together with the war it brought an as-yet-unseen bitterness and coarsening in all, without exception, strata of Russian people. A whole series of other circumstances leads to a situation wherein, no matter how we should strain toward the preservation of culture, a time of temporary decline and tarnishing of culture lies ahead. Together with culture the image of Pushkin will also tarnish.

But I would be insincere if, having once started talking of this, I did not express myself to the end. It may happen that the general twilight of our culture should disperse, but that phenomenon which I have called the eclipse of Pushkin will yet last longer and will not pass without leaving its mark. The historical rupture with the previous, Pushkinian epoch, will forever move Pushkin away into the depths of history. That closeness to Pushkin within which we grew up shall never again repeat itself...

Pushkin did not value popular adoration, for he did not believe in it. At best he had hoped to be liked by the people "for a long time"—but not "forever." "And long shall I remain liked by the people..." He saw the process of cooling-off as unavoidable, and outwardly expressed in two ways: either the crowd spits at the altar of the poet, that is, insults and hates him—or else it shakes his tripod in "childlike playfulness." In relation to Push-kin himself the first formula is already impossible: the "crowd" will never spit at the altar where his fire yet burns; but the next line: "And in childlike playfulness it shakes your tripod," will fully come to pass. We are already watching the advent of the second eclipse. And there will be more of them. The tripod will not fall for all ages, but it will be periodically shaken under the surging pressure of the crowd, which, playful and pitying nothing, is like history, like time. This is the "playful child" to whom no one will know how to say: "Stop! Don't fool around."

Time drives the crowd of people, who hurry to climb up on the stage of history, in order to play their role...and relinquish their place to others who are already shoving from behind. Making noise and crowding around, the mass shakes the tripod of the poet. We throw our most valuable possessions, our love for Pushkin, like a handful of sweet-smelling grass, into the fire of the tripod. And it will burn.

Moved back into the "smoke of centuries," Pushkin will arise in gigantic stature. National pride in him will flow into indestructible bronze forms—but that spontaneous closeness, that heart-felt tenderness with which *we* loved Pushkin will never be known to coming generations. They will not be granted this joy. They will never see the face of Pushkin as we have seen it. This mysterious face, the face of a demigod, will change, in the very manner that it sometimes seems the bronze face of a statue changes. And who knows what it is that coming people will read on it, what discoveries they will make in the world that was cre-ated by Pushkin? Perhaps they will solve the riddles that we did not solve. But much of what was seen and loved by *us* they will never see.

That which I have spoken about is probably felt by many as a burning anguish, as something horrific, from which one may, perhaps, want to hide. Perhaps I too feel the pain, and I too feel like hiding—but what is to be done? History, generally speaking, *is* uncomfortable. "And from the fates there's no protection."

The heightened interest in the words of the poet which was

felt by many people during the past several years arose, perhaps, from a premonition, from an insistent need: partly to decipher Pushkin while it is not yet too late, while the tie with his time is not yet lost forever; and partly, it seems to me, it was suggested by the same premonition: we are agreeing to what call we should answer, how we should communicate with each other in the oncoming darkness.

Translated by Alexander Golubov

Alexander Blok

ON THE MISSION OF THE POET

Ever since childhood we have kept in memory a cheerful name: Pushkin. It is a name, a sound which has filled many days of our lives. Somber names of emperors, generals, inventors of instruments of murder, names of torturers and martyrs of life; and together with them, this radiant name: Pushkin.

Pushkin was able to bear his creative burden easily and cheerfully, although the poet's role is not an easy and cheerful one; it is tragic. Pushkin executed his role with sweeping confidence and panache, like a great master. But often our hearts contract in pain at the thought of Pushkin: the festive, triumphal procession of a poet who could not hinder the outer world, for his endeavor—culture—was an inward endeavor—this procession was disturbed all too often by the grim interference of people for whom a stove-pot is more precious than God.

We know Pushkin the man, Pushkin the friend of monarchy, Pushkin the friend of the Decembrists. All this pales before one thing: Pushkin the poet.

The poet is an invariable quantity. His language and devices may become outdated, but the essence of his endeavor does not.

People may turn away from the poet and his endeavor. Today they erect monuments to him; tomorrow they want to "throw him off the ship of modernity." Both actions characterize only the people who engage in them, not the poet—the essence of poetry, as of any art, is invariable; both attitudes of people towards poetry are, in the final analysis, immaterial.

Today we honor the memory of a most eminent Russian poet. In connection with this occasion it seems fitting for me to speak on the *mission of the poet* and to underpin my words with Pushkin's thoughts.

What is a poet? A person who writes in verse? Of course not. He is called a poet not because he writes in verse—he writes in verse, that is, he harmonizes words and sounds, because he is a son of harmony, a poet.

What is harmony? Harmony is the consonance of world forces, the order of world life. Order is cosmos, in distinction to disorder—chaos. Cosmos is born of chaos, as the ancients taught. Cosmos is akin to chaos, just as the springy waves of the sea are akin to heaps of ocean billows. A son can be unlike his father in everything save for one secret trait; but it is this trait that makes father and son alike.

Chaos is primordial, elemental anarchy; cosmos—ordered harmony and culture; from chaos arises cosmos; the element harbors seeds of culture; from anarchy harmony is created.

World life consists of the never-ending creation of new species, new races. They are lulled by anarchic chaos; culture nurtures and selects among them; harmony imparts to them images and forms that dissolve again into the anarchic mist. The meaning of this is incomprehensible to us, the essence of this, obscure; we console ourselves with the thought that a new race is better than an old one; but the wind extinguishes this small candle wherewith we try to illuminate the world night. The order of the world is disturbing; it is the child of disorder and may not coincide with our ideas on what is good and what is bad.

We do know one thing: that a race which supplants another one is new, and that the race which it supplants is old; we observe an eternal flux in the world; we ourselves participate in the flux of races; for the most part our participation is inactive: we degenerate, grow old, and die; occasionally it is active: we occupy some place in world culture and personally contribute to the formation of new races.

The poet is a son of harmony, and he is granted a role in world culture. Three labors are incumbent upon him: first, to liberate sounds from the native anarchic element in which they dwell; second, to harmonize these sounds and give them form; third, to bring this harmony into the outer world.

Sounds that have been snatched from the element, harmonized, and brought into the world begin to perform their labor themselves. "The poet's words are already his deeds." They display unexpected might; they test human hearts and make a selection among the heaps of human dross; perhaps they collect some parts of the old race that bears the name "man," parts suitable for the creation of new races, since the old one, evidently, is quickly waning, degenerating, and dying.

The might of harmony brought by poetry into the world is irresistible; struggle with it exceeds both personal and combined human powers. "If only all were as susceptible to the power of harmony!" agonizes lonely Salieri. But all are susceptible to it, only mortals differently from a god—Mozart. From the mark that poetry makes in passing, from the name that it gives—no one can escape, just as no one can escape from death. This name is given unerringly.

Thus, for example, those who are a simple fragment of the element, those who are unable and not privileged to understand, will never deserve a bad name from the poet. People who are like the earth which they till, like the wisp of fog from which they come, like the beast which they hunt, are not called rabble. Contrariwise, those who do not wish to understand, although they should understand many things, for they too serve culture—such people are branded with a shameful label: *rabble*. Not even death saves one from this label; the label remains even after death, just as it remained on Count Beckendorff, Timkovsky, and Bulgarin— on all those who have hindered the poet from fulfilling his mission.

Upon the fathomless depths of the spirit where man ceases to be man, on depths inaccessible to state and society created by civilization, roll waves of sound that are like the waves of aether encompassing the universe; rhythmical fluctuations occur there that are like the processes forming mountains, winds, sea currents, and the animal and vegetable world.

This depth of spirit is concealed by phenomena of the outer world. Pushkin says that it may be concealed more from the poet than from other people: "Among the worthless children of the world he is perhaps the most worthless of all."

The first labor demanded of the poet by his service is to forsake "the cares of the bustling world" in order to raise the outer covers and reveal the depth. This demand elevates the poet above the "worthless children of the world."

> He runs, frantic and grim,
> Full of sounds and perturbation,
> To the desolate sea-strand,
> Into widely-rustling oak groves.

Frantic, grim, and full of perturbation, because the revelation of spiritual depth is just as difficult as the act of birth. To the sea and into the forest, because only there can one muster all of one's strength in solitude and commune with the "native chaos," the anarchic element rolling waves of sound.

The mysterious labor is consummated; the cover removed, the depth revealed, the sound received into the soul. Apollo's second demand is that the sound which is raised from the depth and foreign to the outer world be couched in the enduring and tangible form of the word; sounds and words must constitute a single harmony. This is the field of master craftsmanship. It demands inspiration, just as communion with the "dear, inborn chaos" does. "Inspiration," said Pushkin, "is the propensity of the soul to a most vivid reception of impressions and understanding of concepts, and consequently, to their explanation." Therefore, no precise boundaries between the poet's first and second labor can be drawn; one is completely connected with the other. The more covers that are raised, the more intense the communion with chaos, the more difficult the birth of a sound—the clearer the form it strives to assume, the more prolonged and harmonious it is, the more doggedly it pursues human hearing.

The turn comes for the poet's third labor: sounds that have been received into the soul and harmonized must be brought into the world. Here there occurs the notorious clash of

75

the poet with the rabble.

The common folk were hardly ever called rabble. Surely only those who deserved this label themselves applied it to the common people. Pushkin collected folk songs and wrote in the folk manner; he felt very close to his country nanny. Therefore, one must be a dull or malicious person to think that Pushkin could have meant the common folk when he used the term "rabble." A Pushkin dictionary will clear up this matter—if Russian culture is reborn.

By "rabble" Pushkin meant approximately the same thing that we do. He often affixed to this noun the epithet "society," thus giving a collective name to the hereditary nobles of the court who were devoid of everything save their aristocratic titles. But even before Pushkin's eyes the hereditary nobility was quickly giving way to the bureaucracy. These bureacrats are our rabble; the rabble of yesterday and today: not nobility, not common folk; not beasts, not clods of earth, not wisps of fog, not chunks of planets, not demons and not angels. Without the addition of the particle "not" only one thing can be said of them: they are people. This is not particularly flattering; people are self-seekers and vulgarians whose spiritual depth is hopelessly and lastingly concealed by the "cares of the bustling world."

The rabble demand that the poet serve the same thing which they serve: the outer world. They demand "usefulness" of him, as Pushkin simply puts it; they demand that the poet "sweep garbage off the street," "enlighten the hearts of his fellowmen," and so on.

From their point of view the rabble are right in their demands. First, they will never be able to enjoy the fruits of that small amount of labor beyond street-sweeping that is demanded of the poet. Second, they instinctively feel that this labor, one way or another, quickly or slowly, leads to their detriment. The testing of hearts with harmony is not a quiet pursuit ensuring the rabble's desired, equable course of events in the outer world.

The class of rabble, like other human classes, incidentally, progresses very slowly. Thus, for example, although human brains have swelled up to the detriment of all the other functions of the organism, people have hit upon the idea of setting apart from the state only one organ—censorship—to safeguard the order of their world, which expresses itself in state forms. In this fashion they have set up a barrier only on the poet's third path—the path of bringing harmony into the world. It would seem that they could have thought of setting up barriers on the first and second paths too; they could have found means to roil the very wellsprings of harmony. What it is that restrains them—lack of imagination, timidity, or conscience—we do not know. But perhaps such means are already being sought?

However, the poet's endeavor, as we have seen, is quite incommensurate with the order of the outer world. The poet's tasks, as we are accustomed to saying, are cultural; his endeavor is historical. Therefore, the poet has the right to repeat after Pushkin:

> It's small grief to me if the press fools
> Blockheads freely, or if vigilant censorship
> Constrains a wag's journalistic schemes.

Speaking thus, Pushkin confirmed the rabble's right to establish censorship, for he believed that the number of blockheads would not diminish.

The poet's endeavor is assuredly not to get through without fail to all blockheads; rather, the harmony he achieves selects among them in order to extract something more interesting than the ordinary run of mankind from the heap of human dross. This goal, of course, will be attained sooner or later by true harmony; no censorship in the world can hinder this fundamental endeavor of poetry.

Let us not argue, on a day devoted to Pushkin's memory, about whether he correctly or incorrectly divided the freedom we call personal from the freedom we call political. We know that he demanded a "different," "secret" freedom. In our opinion, it is "personal," but for the poet it is not only personal freedom:

> To be
> Accountable to no man; to serve and
> Please oneself alone; for power or livery
> Not to bend one's conscience, ideas, and neck;
> To wander here and there at one's *caprice,*
> Marvelling at Nature's divine beauties,
> And to melt silently in rapturous joy
> Before the works of art and inspiration—
> That is happiness! Those are rights!

This was said not long before he died. In his youth Pushkin spoke about the same thing:

> Love and *secret freedom* have inspired
> A simple hymn within my heart.

This *secret freedom,* this *caprice*—the message which Fet ("The bard of mad caprice!") later repeated most loudly of all—is not only personal freedom, but a much greater one: it is closely connected with the first two labors that Apollo demands of the poet. Everything enumerated in Pushkin's verse is the *sine qua non* for the liberation of harmony. Though permitting interference in the labor of testing people with harmony—the third labor—Pushkin could not permit interference in the first two labors; and these labors are not personal.

Meanwhile, as Pushkin's life drew to a close, it filled up more and more with barriers set up on his paths. Pushkin grew weak—and with him the culture of his time—the only period of culture in Russia of the last century—grew weak too. The fateful forties were drawing nigh; over Pushkin's deathbed Belinsky drooled his childish babble. This babble seemed to us completely antithetical and completely hostile to the suave voice of Count Beckendorff. It seems to us to be so even now. It would be too painful to us all if it turned out that this is not so. And, even if this is not quite so, we shall think anyway that this is not so at all. For it still holds true that:

An elevating illusion is dearer to us
Than a host of lowly truths.

In the second half of the century Pisarev was already shouting at the top of his lungs what was heard in Belinsky's childish babble.

I shall refrain from further comparisons, for it is still impossible to make the picture clear; perhaps behind the cobweb of time something will be revealed that is completely different from what runs through my rambling thoughts and from what is firmly implanted in thoughts opposite to mine. We must still experience some events; the verdict on this matter rests in the hands of a future historian of Russia.

Pushkin is dead. But "for boys Posas do not die," said Schiller. And Pushkin too was not killed at all by d'Anthes' bullet. He was killed by lack of air. His culture was dying with him.

It's time, my friend, it's time! The heart asks for peace.

These were the sighs that Pushkin vented before his death, and also the sighs of the culture of Pushkin's time.

In the world there is no happiness,
But there is peace and liberty.

Peace and *liberty*. They are indispensable to the poet for the freeing of harmony. But peace and liberty are also being taken away. Not outer peace, but creative peace. Not liberty to misbehave, not freedom to play the liberal, but creative liberty— the secret freedom. And the poet dies because he is stifled; life has lost its meaning.

The amiable bureaucrats who have hindered the poet in testing hearts with harmony will always bear the label "rabble."

But they have hindered the poet in his third labor only. The testing of hearts with Pushkin's poetry in all its scope has already been accomplished without them.

Let those bureaucrats who plan to direct poetry through their own channels, violating its secret freedom and hindering it in fulfilling its mysterious mission, let them beware of an even worse label.

We die, but art remains. Its ultimate purposes are unknown to us and cannot be known. It is one in substance and indivisible.

And for fun, I should like to proclaim three simple truths:

There are no special arts; the name of art should not be given to what is not properly art; in order to create works of art, one must know how to do it.

In these cheerful truths of common sense, before which we are so sinful, one may swear by the cheerful name of Pushkin.

Translated by Joel Stern

Boris Pasternak

SOME STATEMENTS

1

When I talk about mysticism, or painting, or the theater, I talk in that peaceable and unconstrained way in which any freely thinking reader considers things. When the talk turns to literature, I remember the book itself and become unable to consider things rationally. I have to be shaken awake and brought by force from a physical condition of dreaming about the book, as if from a swoon, and only then, and only with great reluctance, overcoming a slight revulsion, will I join in a conversation on any other literary subject, where the issue is not a book but something else, no matter what: public readings, say, or poets, or schools, or new developments in the arts, and so forth. But not for anything would I ever move of my own free will, uncompelled, out of the world of what deeply interests me, into this world of amateurs taking an interest.

2

Contemporary trends of thought imagine that art is like a fountain, whereas it is a sponge. They have decided that art should gush forth, whereas it should absorb and become saturated. They think it can be broken down into methods of depiction, whereas it is composed of organs of perception. The proper task of art is to be always an observer, to gaze more purely than others do, more receptively and faithfully, but in our time it has become acquainted with powder and the make-up room, and displays itself from a stage; as if there were two kinds of art in the world, and one of them, having the other in reserve, can permit itself the luxury of self-distortion, a luxury equivalent to suicide. It shows itself off, while it ought to be sunk in obscurity, in the back rows , hardly aware that its hat is aflame on its head, or that, though it has hidden away in a corner, it is stricken with a phosphorescence and a light-transparency, as with some kind of illness.

3

A book is a cubic piece of burning, smoking conscience—and nothing else.

Mating calls are the care nature takes to preserve the feathered species, her vernal ringing in the ears. A book is like a woodgrouse calling in the spring. Deafened with its own sound, listening spellbound to itself, it hears nothing and nobody. Without it, the spiritual race would have had no continuation. It would have become extinct. Monkeys had no books.

A book is written. It grows, it gathers experience, it knocks about the world, and now it's grown up and—this is what it is. It is not to blame for the fact that we can see right through it. That's how the spiritual universe is arranged. Yet not very long ago the scenes in a book were thought to be dramatizations. This is wrong—what should it want them for? People forgot that the only thing which lies in our power is to know how not to distort the voice of life that sounds within us.

Inability to find and tell the truth is a deficiency that cannot be covered up by any amount of ability to tell untruths. A book is a living being. It is quite conscious and in its right mind: its pictures and scenes are what it has brought out of the past and committed to memory, and is not prepared to forget.

4

Life hasn't just begun. Art never had a beginning. Always, until the moment of its stopping, it was constantly there.

It is infinite. It is here, at this moment, behind me and inside me, and, as if the doors of an Assembly Hall were suddenly flung open, I am immersed in its fresh, headlong omnilocality and omnitemporality, as if an oath of allegiance were to be sworn without delay.

No genuine book has a first page. Like the rustling of a forest, it is begotten God knows where, and it grows and it rolls, arousing the dense wilds of the forest until suddenly, in the very darkest, most stunned and panicked moment, it rolls to its end and begins to speak with all the tree-tops at once.

5

What is a miracle? It is that once upon a time there lived on earth a seventeen-year-old girl called Mary Stuart, and one October day, at her little window, with the Puritans jeering outside, she wrote a poem in French which ended with these words:

> *Car mon pis et mon mieux*
> *Sont les plus déserts lieux.*

Secondly, it is that once upon a time, in his youth, at a window with October carousing and raving outside, the English poet Charles Algernon Swinburne finished his "Chastelard," in which the quiet plaint of Mary's five stanzas was thought up into the uncanny booming of five tragic acts.

Thirdly, finally, it is that once, about five years ago, when a translator glanced through the window, he did not know which thing to find more amazing—the way the Yelabuga blizzard knew

Scottish and, just as on that day, was distressed about the seventeen-year-old girl; or the way that girl and the English poet, her sorrower, had been able to tell him so well, so intimately, in Russian, what was still troubling them both as before and still pursuing them.

What does this mean?—the translator asked himself. What is going on over there? Why is it so quiet there today (and yet so stormy!)? It would seem that, because we're sending there, someone ought to be bleeding to death. And yet they are smiling there.

This is what a miracle is. It is the unity and identity of these three lives and of a whole host of others (bystanders and witnesses of three epochs—people, biographies, readers) in the authentic October of who knows what years, booming, and blinded and growing hoarse, out there beyond the window, beneath the mountain—in art.

This is what it is.

6

Misunderstandings exist. They have to be avoided. Here there is room for boredom. A writer, people say, a poet...

Aesthetics does not exist. It seems to me that aesthetics doesn't exist as a punishment for the way it lies, pardons, panders, condescends. For the way, while knowing nothing about man, it spins its gossip about specialist subjects. Portraitists, landscapists, genre painter, still-life painter? Symbolist, acmeist, futurist? What murderous jargon!

Clearly this is a science that classifies air balloons according to where and how the holes are placed in them, which interfere with their flying.

Inseparable from each other, poetry and prose are two opposite poles.

By its inborn faculty of hearing, poetry seeks out the melody of nature amid the tumult of the dictionary, and then, picking it up as one picks up a tune, abandons itself to improvization upon that theme. By scent, and according to its level of inspiration, prose seeks and finds the human being in the category of speech, and if the age is deprived of him, it recreates him from memory, secretly abandons him, and then, for the good of mankind, pretends it has found him in the midst of the contemporary world. These principles do not exist in isolation.

As it weaves its fantasies, poetry stumbles across nature. The live, real world is the only project of the imagination, which, having once succeeded, goes on forever, endlessly succeeding. Look at it continuing, moment after moment a success. It is still real, still deep, absorbing, fascinating. It is not something you'll be disappointed in next morning. For the poet it is an example, even more than a model or pattern.

7

It is madness to trust in common sense. It is madness to doubt it. It is madness to look ahead. It is madness to live without looking. But now and then to roll your eyes and, with your blood temperature rapidly rising, to hear how, stroke upon stroke, reminiscent of convulsions of lightnings on dusty ceilings and plaster casts, there begins to expand and resound, along your consciousness, the reflected mural of some sort of unearthly, rapidly passing, eternally spring-like thunderstorm—this is *pure* madness, surely the very purest madness!

It is natural to strive for purity.

And so we go right up to the pure essence of poetry. It is disturbing, like the ominous turning of a dozen windmills at the edge of a bare field in a black year of famine.

Translated by Angela Livingstone

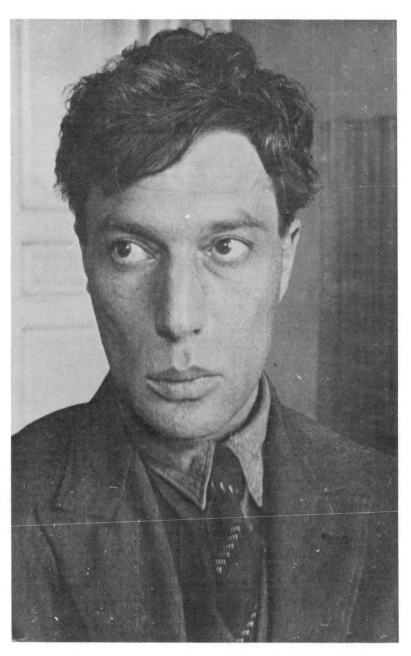

Pasternak, 1918

from *A SAFE-CONDUCT*

Although my story has inclined this way, I have not asked
the question of what music is or what leads up to it. I haven't
done so, not only because I woke up one night in my third year of
life and found the horizon flooded with it for more than fifteen
years ahead, and thus had no occasion to experience its problem-
atics, but also because it now ceases to bear on our theme. However, the same question in relation to art as such, art as a whole, in
other words in relation to poetry, cannot be passed over. I shall
answer it neither theoretically nor in a sufficiently general form,
but much of what I shall relate will be the answer I can give for
myself and for my poet.

The sun used to rise behind the post-office and, slipping
down Kiselny Street, would set over Neglinka. When it had gilded
our part of the house, it would make its way from lunchtime on
into the dining room and kitchen. The flat was government proper-
ty; its rooms were made up from classrooms. I was studying at the
University. I was reading Hegel and Kant. It was a time when, at
every meeting with friends, gulfs would yawn open and now one,
now another of us would put forward some newly revealed discovery.

Often we would get each other up in the dead of night. The
reason for it always seemed of utmost urgency. Whoever was
woken was ashamed of his sleep, as if it was an accidentally ex-
posed weakness. To the fright of the unfortunate inhabitants of
the house, all without exception considered nonentities, we would
instantly set off—as if to an adjoining room—to Sokol'niki, the
Yaroslavl railway crossing. I had made friends with a girl from a
wealthy family. It was obvious to everyone that I loved her. She
only took part in these walks in the abstract, on the lips of those

more used to going without sleep and adapted to such a life. I was giving a few meagerly paid lessons so as not to take money from my father. In the summers, when my family went away, I used to stay in the town at my own expense. The illusion of independence was obtained by means of such moderation in food, that on top of everything else there was hunger too, which conclusively transformed night into day in the uninhabited flat. Music, which I was still just putting off saying goodbye to, was already becoming interwoven with literature. The depth and charm of Bely and Blok could not but be revealed to me. Their influence was combined in a singular way with a force that went beyond mere ignorance. My fifteen-year abstinence from words, which I had sacrificed to sounds, doomed me to originality as a certain kind of maiming dooms a person to acrobatics. Along with some of my acquaintances I had connections with Musaget. From others I learnt of the existence of Marburg. Kant and Hegel were replaced by Cohen, Natorp and Plato.

I am characterizing my life of those years with intentional randomness. I could multiply these tokens or exchange them for others. However, the ones I have given are enough for my purpose. Using them to mark out approximately—as on a technical sketch— what reality was for me at that time, I shall ask myself at this point by what virtue, and where in it, poetry was born. I shall not have to spend long over the answer. This is the only feeling memory has preserved in all its freshness.

It was born from the interruptions of these orders of things, from the diversity of their speed, from the way the more sluggish lagged behind and piled up far in the rear, on the deep horizon of memory.

Love raced along most impetuously of all. Sometimes it found itself at the head of nature, and would overtake the sun. But as this happened only rarely, one could say that the force which gilded one side of the house and then began to bronze the other, which washed weather away with weather and turned the heavy winch of the four seasons, moved forward with constant superiority, nearly always competing with love. While at the back, at various distances, the remaining orders dragged along. I often heard the hiss of a yearning that had not begun with me. Catching up with me from behind, it made me feel frightened and pitying. It issued from the point at which everyday life had got torn away, and it either threatened to put brakes on the real, or else begged for everyday life to be joined to the living air, which in the meantime had gone a long way ahead. And what is known as inspiration consisted in this turning round to look back. The most tumid, uncreative parts of existence called for a special vividness because of the distance to which they had rolled away. Inanimate objects acted still more strongly. They were models for a still-life, a branch of art especially beloved of artists. Piling up in the very furthest distance of the living universe, and being in a state of immobility, they provided the fullest possible idea of it as a moving entirety, as any limit does that seems to us a contrast. Their disposition marked a frontier beyond which wonder and pity had nothing to do. There, science was at work, seeking the atomic foundations of reality.

But since there was no second universe from which one could have lifted reality up out of the first, taking it by its tops as if by the hair, the manipulations it itself called for required that a representation of it be taken, as in algebra which, in the realm of quantity, is straitened by just the same singleness of plane. But to me this representation always seemed a way out of the difficulty, not an aim in itself. I always conceived the aim as being to shift the thing represented from cold axles to hot, to make what had already been lived set off in pursuit of, to catch up, life. This is how I reasoned at that time, not very differently from how I think now. We represent people in order to throw a cloak of weather upon them. Weather—or what is the same thing, nature—we represent in order to throw our passion upon its shoulders. We drag the everyday into prose for the sake of poetry. We draw prose into poetry for the sake of music. This is what, in the broadest sense of the word, I called art, set by the clock of the living race that chimes by the generation.

* * *

There exists a so-called elevated attitude towards women. I shall say a little about this. There is that immense sphere of phenomena which provokes suicides in adolescence. There is the sphere of mistakes made by the infant imagination, of childish perversions and adolescent starvations, the sphere of Kreutzer sonatas and sonatas written against Kreutzer sonatas. I was once in this sphere and stayed in it a shamefully long time. But what *is* it? It tears you to pieces and nothing ever comes of it but harm. And yet there will never be a liberation from it. Everyone who enters history as a human being will always have to go through this. For these sonatas, which are the threshold to the only complete moral freedom, are written not by Tolstoys and Wedekinds but—through their hands—by nature herself. And only in their mutual contradictoriness lies the fullness of her purpose.

Having founded matter upon resistance and divided the factual from the imagined by a dam called love, she takes care to keep this firm, that is, to keep the world entire. Here is the point where her craziness centers, her morbid exaggerations. It can truly be said that here, at every step, she turns a fly into an elephant.

But excuse me—she does make real elephants too! This is said to be her main business. Or is that just a phrase? Well, what about the history of species? And the history of human names? Moreover, the place where she makes them is here, in these sluiced off sections of living evolution, at the dams where her agitated imagination has such free play.

So mayn't it be said that the reason we exaggerate in childhood and have disordered imaginations is that at that time we are flies and nature is making elephants of us?

Holding to the philosophy that only the *almost impossible* is real, she has made feeling extraordinarily difficult for everything alive. She has made it difficult for the animal in one way, in another way for the plant. The way she has made it difficult for us shows her astoundingly high opinion of man. She has made it difficult for us not through any sort of mechanical tricks, but through what she considers has absolute power for us. She has made it difficult for us through the sense of our fly-like vulgarity, which seizes each one of us the more strongly, the further we are from the fly. This is stated with genius by Andersen in his "Ugly Duckling."

All literature about sex, like the word "sex" itself, smacks of an exasperating vulgarity, and in this lies its purpose. It is solely and precisely through this repulsiveness that it is useful to nature, for her contact with us is founded on this very fear of vulgarity, and anything not vulgar would fail to strengthen her means of control.

Whatever material our thoughts might supply in this connection, the *fate* of that material is in her hands. And by means of the instinct which she has detailed to us out of all her entirety, nature always manages that material in such a way that all efforts of pedagogues, directed as they are towards making it easier to be natural, invariably make it harder, and *this is just how it ought to be.*

This is necessary in order that feeling itself should have something to overcome. If not dumbfounded one way, then another way. And it doesn't matter *what* nastiness or nonsense the barrier is built up of. The movement that leads to conception is the purest movement out of all those known to the universe. And this purity alone, which has triumphed so many times in the course of the centuries, is enough to make everything which is not it seem by contrast infinitely dirty.

And there is art. Art is concerned not with man but with the image of man. But the image of man, it turns out, is bigger than man. It can have its conception only in motion and even then not in just any. It can have its conception only in the transition from fly to elephant.

What is it the honest man does when he speaks *only* the truth? While he is telling the truth time goes by; in that time life moves ahead. His truth lags behind, it deceives. Is this the way man must speak, everywhere and always?

And so in art his mouth is shut for him. In art the man falls silent and the image begins to speak. And it turns out that *only* the image can keep pace with the progress of nature.

In Russian "to lie" *(vrat')* means *to say the superfluous,* rather than *to deceive.* It is in this sense that art lies. Its image encompasses life and does not seek a spectator. Its truths are not depictive but are capable of eternal development.

Only *art*, speaking for centuries about love, is not at the disposal of the instinct for strengthening the means of impeding feeling. A generation, when it has taken the hurdle of a new spiritual development, *preserves* the lyric truth, and does not reject it, so that from a very big distance one might imagine mankind to be gradually composing itself from the generations in the forms of lyric truth.

All this is extraordinary. All this is breathtakingly difficult. Taste teaches morality, but power teaches taste.

* * *

There exists a psychology of creation, the problems of poetics. Meanwhile what is experienced most immediately of all in the whole of art is precisely its coming into being, and about this there is no need to make guesses.

We cease to recognize reality. It presents itself in some new category. This category seems to us to be its, not our, condition. Except for this condition everything in the world has been named. It alone is unnamed and new. We try to name it. The result is art.

The clearest, most memorable and most important thing in art is its origination, and the world's best works of art, while telling about the most various things, are really telling about their own birth....

At the beginning of *A Safe-Conduct* I said that sometimes love outstripped the sun. I had in mind that patency of feeling which every morning outdistanced the whole of the surrounding world with the reliability of a piece of news that has just been confirmed anew for the hundredth time. In comparison with this, even the sunrise acquired the character of a local rumor still needing verification. In other words, I had in mind the patency of a power which outweighed the patency of light.

If, given the knowledge, abilities and leisure, I were to decide now to write a creative aesthetics, I would construct it upon two concepts—upon the concepts of power and symbol. I would show that as distinct from science, which takes nature in the section of a shaft of light, art is interested in life at the moment when the ray of power *is passing through it*. I would take the concept of power, or force, in that widest sense in which it is taken by theoretical physics, only with the difference that it would be a question not of the principle of power but of its voice, its presence. I would explain that in the context of self-awareness power is called feeling.

When we suppose that in *Tristan, Romeo and Juliet* and other great memorable works a powerful passion is portrayed, we underestimate their content. Their theme is wider than this powerful theme. Their theme is the theme of power.

And it is from this theme that art is born. Art is more one-sided than people think. It cannot be directed at will, wherever you wish, like a telescope. Focussed upon a reality that has been displaced by feeling, art is a record of this displacement. It copies it from nature. How then does nature become displaced? Details gain in sharpness, each losing its independent meaning. Each one of them could be replaced by another. Any one of them is precious. Any one, chosen at random, will serve as evidence of the state which envelops the whole of transposed reality.

When the signs of this condition are transferred onto paper the characteristics of life become the characteristics of creation. The latter stand out more sharply than the former. They have been better studied. There is a terminology for them. They are called devices.

Art is realistic, as activity, and it is symbolic, as fact. It is realistic by virtue of the fact that it did not itself invent metaphor but found it in nature and faithfully reproduced it. The transferred sense means nothing in isolation, but refers to the general spirit of all art, just as the parts of the transposed reality mean nothing if taken separately.

And in the configuration of its whole, art is symbolic. Its only symbol is in the sharpness and non-obligatoriness of images, which is characteristic of it *as a whole*. The interchangeability of images is the sign of the situation in which the parts of reality are mutually indifferent. The interchangeability of images, that is, art, is the symbol of power.

Properly, only power needs the language of material proofs. The other aspects of consciousness are durable without any signs. For them there is the direct path to the visual analogies of light: to number, to the exact notion, to the idea. But there is nothing, except the mobile language of images, that is, the language of accompanying signs, for power to express itself by, the fact of power, power which lasts only for the moment of its manifestation.

The direct speech of feeling is allegorical and there is nothing by which it can be replaced.

* * *

The time and the sharing of influences made me akin to Mayakovsky. There were coincidences between us. I had noticed them. I realized that if I did not do something about myself, they would occur more often in the future. I had to protect him from their vulgarity. Though I could not have given it a name, I resolved to renounce everything that led to them. I renounced the Romantic manner. This was how the unromantic poetic style of *Over the Barriers* came into being.

But a whole conception of life lay concealed beneath the Romantic manner which I was to forbid myself from henceforth. This was the conception of life as the life of the poet. It had come to us from the Symbolists and had been adopted by them from the Romantics, principally the Germans.

Blok had been possessed by this idea but only for a certain time. In the form in which it came to him naturally, it was incapable of satisfying him. He had either to heighten it or to abandon it altogether. He abandoned the idea, Mayakovsky and Esenin heightened it.

In the poet who lays himself down as the measure of life,

and pays for this with his life, the Romantic conception is irresistibly vivid and irrefutable in its symbols, that is in everything that figuratively touches upon Orphism and Christianity. In this sense something not transient was incarnate in the life of Mayakovsky and also in the fate of Esenin, a fate which defies all epithets, self-destructively begging to become myth and receding into it. But outside the legend, the Romantic scheme is false. The poet, who is its foundation, is inconceivable without the non-poets to bring him into relief, for this poet is not a living personality absorbed in moral cognition, but a visual-biographical 'emblem' which demands a background to make its contours visible. In contra-distinction to the Passion Plays, which needed a Heaven in order to be heard, this drama needs the evil of mediocrity to be seen, as Romanticism always needs philistinism, and with the disappearance of the petty bourgeoisie loses half its content.

The notion of biography as spectacle was inherent in my time. I shared this notion with everyone else. I abandoned it while it was still optional and mild among the Symbolists, before it began to imply heroism and before it smelt of blood. And in the first place, I freed myself from it unconsciously, abandoning the Romantic devices for which it served as basis. In the second place, I also shunned it consciously, as a brilliance unsuited to me because, confining myself to my craft, I feared any kind of poeticizing which would place me in a false and incongruous position.

But when *My Sister Life* appeared, a book in which were expressed wholly uncontemporary aspects of poetry, revealed to me in the revolutionary summer, I became utterly indifferent as to the name of the power that had given me the book, because it was immensely bigger than me and the poetic conception surrounding me.

Translated by Angela Livingstone

Boris Pasternak

from *NOTES OF A TRANSLATOR*

I

Translations either have no meaning at all, or else must have a closer relation to their originals than is usually supposed. Correspondence of text to text is too weak a link to guarantee a translation's expediency. Such translations fail to do what they promise. Their pale re-tellings convey no sense of the most important thing about the object they undertake to reflect—its power. To achieve this aim, a translation has to be connected with its original by a more real dependence. The relation between an original and a translation must be the relation between a function and its derivative, between a tree-trunk and the new shoot struck from it. A translation must come from an author who has experienced the influence of the original upon himself long before he starts work. It must be the fruit of the original and its historical consequence.

This is why imitations and borrowings, the products of a school and instances of foreign influence lead more intimately into the world of European models than do the direct transpositions of those models. What the present anthology does is offer a picture of such influences. It portrays English poetry from the point of view of the power we have experienced from it. It shows English poetry in its Russian effect. This corresponds in the highest degree to the very idea of translation, its very purpose.

We have already said that translations are unrealizable because the chief charm of a work of art lies in its unrepeatability. So how can a translation repeat it?

Translations are conceivable because ideally they too must be works of art, and must, by virtue of their own unrepeatability, stand on the same level as the originals, even while sharing their text. Translations are conceivable because for centuries before our time whole literatures have translated one another; translations are not a method of becoming acquainted with individual works, but a medium for the age-old intercourse of cultures and peoples.

*

The possibilities of English meter are inexhaustible. The non-polysyllabic nature of the English language opens up the most lavish space to the English syllable. The compactness of the English phrase is a pledge of its richness in content, and richness in content is a guarantee of musicality, because the music of a word consists not in its euphony but in the correlation between its sound and its meaning. In this sense English versification is supremely musical.

Once we vainly tried to explain Pushkin's and Lermontov's youthful anglomania solely as the influence of Byron's ideas. We always sensed some other, elusive, foundation to their enthusiasm. Later, when we gained a modest acquaintance with Keats and Swinburne, we were arrested by the same enigma. The measure of our delight was not accounted for by the attraction they themselves exerted. Beyond their effect upon us we seemed to catch sight of that same additional mysterious something, repeated once more. For a long time we attributed this phenomenon to the fascination of the English language itself and to the advantages it offers to lyric poetry. We were wrong. The secret additional something that gives a supplementary charm to every English line is the invisible presence of Shakespeare and his influence in a whole host of the most effective and typical devices and turns of phrase in English.

Very recently the editors of the *Anthology* decided that it could not be published while it contained no translations from Shelley. To make up this deficiency they turned to Akhmatova, Zenkevich and the present writer.

Despite editorial prejudice and opposition we still think that the Russian Shelley was and is the three-volume Balmont translation. In its time this work was a discovery similar to those made by Zhukovsky. The neglect it has received is based on a misunderstanding. Balmont's work on Shelley coincided with the creative years of his youth, when his fresh originality was not yet spoiled by the later watery artificiality. It is a great shame that the later Balmont uncrowns the earlier one.

With extreme reluctance, we addressed ourselves to a poet whom we had always found distant and abstract, foreseeing no joy from the task. Quite likely we were right and our translations are unsuccessful. But we should never have completed them had we kept our previous opinion of that great lyric poet. In order to get close to him, even at the price of failure, we had to look at him a little more intently. We arrived at an unexpected conception.

In this invoker of the elements, this singer of revolutions, this atheist and author of atheistic treatises, we discovered a precursor and herald of the urbanistic mysticism which later pervaded Russian and European Symbolism. And no sooner had we caught the future voices of Blok, Verhaeren and Rilke in Shelley's apostrophes to clouds and wind, than everything in him took on flesh for us. Naturally, we still translated him as a classical poet. These remarks refer chiefly to the "Ode to the West Wind."

II

Shakespeare will always be the favorite of generations which have lived through a great deal and are historically mature. Numerous ordeals teach one to value the voice of facts, real knowledge of things, and the art of realism, which is rich in content and not disposed to joking.

Shakespeare remains the ideal and the high point of this trend. In no one else does knowledge of man attain such a level of rightness, and no one else has set out that knowledge with so much wilfulness. At first glance, these seem contradictory qualities. But they are joined by a direct dependence on each other.

In the first place, this is a miracle of objectivity. There are his famous characters—a gallery of types, ages, temperaments, all with their distinctive types of behavior and their particular modes of speech. And Shakespeare is not disturbed if their conversations are interwoven with the effusions of his own genius. His aesthetics is constructed upon an alternation between self-forgetfulness and attentiveness, between the lofty and the absurd, between prose and verse.

In every respect he is the child of nature: whether we take, say, the unbridled quality of his form, his composition and manner of sculpting, or his psychology, and the moral content of his plays. The explosions of Shakespearean imagery are unsurpassed. His analogies represent the furthest point the subjective principle in poetry has ever reached. He has set a deeper personal imprint on his work than anyone else before or after him.

III

Together with many others, I believe that word-for-word accuracy and formal correspondence are not enough to ensure that a translation will be genuinely close to the original. Just as in the case of a portrait's similarity to what it portrays, the similarity of a translation to the original is achieved by vitality and naturalness of language. No less than original writers the translator must avoid a vocabulary which is not his own in ordinary life and the literary pretence consisting in stylization. Like the original, the translation must produce an impression of life, not literariness.

* *

Shakespeare's use of metaphor, in its insights and its rhetoric, at its peaks and in its troughs, is true to the essence of all genuine allegory.

Metaphorism is the natural consequence of the shortness of man's life and of the vastness of his tasks, planned out for a long time ahead. Because of this discrepancy he is obliged to look at things with eagle-eyed sharpness and to explain himself in momentary illuminations that will be immediately comprehensible. This is what poetry is. Metaphorism is the stenography of a great personality, the shorthand of its soul.

The tempestuous vitality of Rembrandt's, Michelangelo's, Titian's brush is not the result of a carefully considered choice. Assailed by a stormy, insatiable thirst to draw, each one of them, a whole universe, they had no time for any other kind of drawing.

Shakespeare united in himself widely differing stylistic extremes. He combined so many of them that it seems as if there were several authors living inside him. His prose is finished and perfected. It is written by a comic genius with a gift for detail, who possessed the secret of compression and a talent for mimicking everything that is curious and outlandish in the world.

The realm of blank verse in Shakespeare is just the opposite of this. Both Voltaire and Tolstoy found its inner and outer chaos irritating.

Very often a role in Shakespeare will pass through several stages of completion. A character will first speak in scenes that are written in verse, and then he will suddenly burst out in prose. When this happens, the verse scenes give an impression of being preparatory, and the prose scenes one of being final and conclusive.

Verse was Shakespeare's quickest and most immediate form of expression. He had recourse to it as a means of the fastest possible recording of ideas. This goes so far that in many of his verse episodes one discerns rough drafts for prose, done temporarily in verse.

The strength of Shakespeare's poetry lies in its way of being a freely done sketch, which, knowing no restraint, tosses about in powerful disarray.

* * *

Rhythm is the very basis of Shakespeare's poetry. It is the driving force of rhythm that defines the order of questions and answers in his dialogues, the speed of their alternation, the length and brevity of the periods in his monologues.

This rhythm reflects the enviable laconicism of English speech, in which it is possible for one small iambic line to contain a whole statement consisting of one, two, or several propositions set off against each other. It is the rhythm of a free historical personality, which, because it does not set up any idol for itself, is sparing of words and genuine.

Translated by Angela Livingstone

Vladimir Mayakovsky

HOW TO MAKE VERSE

1

I have to write on this subject.

In the course of various literary discussions, in conversation with young workers from various productive literary associations (RAP, TAP, PAP, etc.), in giving short shrift to the critics I often had, if not to destroy, at least to discredit the old poetics. The old poetry itself, which was blameless, was of course left almost intact. It drew fire only when spirited defenders of old junk hid themselves from the new art behind the backsides of monuments.

On the contrary—pulling down the monuments, breaking them up and overturning them, we showed the Great to the readers from a totally unexplored and unknown point of view.

Children (like young literary schools) are always interested in what is inside a cardboard horse. After the work done by the Formalists, the insides of paper horses and elephants are clearly visible. And if the horses have got a bit damaged in the process— sorry! There is no need to quarrel with the poetry of the past— to us it is material for study.

Our chief and unrelenting hatred comes crashing down on the sentimental-critical philistines: on those who see all the greatness of poetry of the past in the fact that they, too, have loved, as Onegin loved Tatyana (souls in harmony!), because they too have an understanding of the poets (they learned them at school!), because iambics caress their ears. We abhor this foolish pandemonium because it creates around the difficult and important craft of poetry an atmosphere of sexual transport and

103

swooning, of belief that immortal poetry alone is not undermined by dialectics and that the only method of production is an inspired throwing back of the head while waiting for the poetry-spirit to descend on one's bald pate in the guise of a dove, a peacock, or an ostrich.

It isn't hard to expose these gentlemen.

It's enough to compare Tatyana's love and "the science sung by Ovid" with the draft marriage laws, to read about Pushkin's "disenchanted lorgnette" to Donetz miners, or to run in front of the column in the May Day parade yelling: "My uncle is of most honest principles!"

It is hardly likely that after such an experiment any youngster burning to dedicate his energies to the revolution would feel a genuine desire to take up the ancient craft of poetry.

Much has been written and said about this. The tumultuous approval of the audience has always been on our side. But straight after this approval sceptical voices were heard:

—You only destroy, and you create NOTHING! Old textbooks are bad, but where are the new ones? Gives us the RULES of your poetics! Give us textbooks!

The excuse that the old poetics has existed for fifteen hundred years, and ours for only thirty, is of little help.

You want to write and you want to know how to do it? Why is a work written according to Shengeli's rules with exact rhymes, iambics and trochees, not accepted as poetry? You have the right to demand that poets should not take the secrets of their craft to their graves.

I want to write about my craft not as a dogmatist but as a practitioner. My article has no scholarly value whatsoever. I am writing about my work, which, according to my observations and convictions, differs very little on the whole from the work of other professional poets.

Once again I must make a very definite reservation: I am not giving any *rules* which will make a man into a poet and enable him to write poetry. Such rules do not exist. The poet is precisely a man who creates these poetic rules for himself.

For the hundredth time I quote my tiresome example and analogy.

A mathematician is a man who creates, amplifies and develops mathematical rules, a man who contributes something new to mathematical knowledge. The man who first formulated "two and two make four" was a great mathematician even if he arrived at that truth by adding two cigarette butts to two more cigarette butts. All those who followed, even if they added much larger things together, for example, a railway engine and another railway engine, are not mathematicians. This assertion in no way detracts from the labor of the man adding up the engines. When transportation is disrupted his labor may be hundreds of times more valuable than the naked arithmetical truth. But one should not send the accounts for railway engine repairs to a mathematical society and demand that they be considered on the same level as Lobachevsky's geometry. This would enrage the planning commission, puzzle the mathematicians, and stump the traffic controllers.

They'll tell me that I am battering my way through a door which is already wide open, that all this is obvious. Nothing of the kind.

Eighty percent of the rhymed trash printed by our publishing houses is printed either because the editors have no understanding of the poetry of the past, or because they don't know what poetry is for.

The editors only know what "I like" or what "I don't like," forgetting that taste, too, can and should be developed. Almost all editors have complained to me that they don't know how to return poetry manuscripts, or what to say when they do.

A competent editor should say to the poet: "Your verses are quite correct, they have been constructed according to the third edition of M. Brodovsky's manual of poetry-writing (or Shengeli's, or Grech's, etc. etc.), all your rhymes are well-tried rhymes, long included in the complete dictionary of Russian rhymes by N. Abramov. Since at present I have no good new verse, I shall willingly take yours, paying what we pay a qualified copyist, three rubles a signature, provided you submit three copies."

The poet will have no recourse. Either he has to give up writing poetry, or he has to approach poetry as a craft which demands more effort. At any rate the poet will stop turning up his nose at the reporter who, for his three rubles per item, does at least report new events. The reporter wears out his pants while following up scandals and fires, while the poet of this kind expends nothing more than saliva—to turn the pages.

For the sake of raising the qualifications of poets and for the sake of the future flowering of poetry, one must stop isolating this easiest of crafts from other types of human labor.

A reservation: the formulation of rules is not in itself the aim of poetry, otherwise the poet could degenerate into a pedant drawing up rules for non-existent or unnecessary things and situations. For example, it is futile to think up rules for counting stars while racing along on a bicycle.

Situations requiring formulation, requiring RULES, are created by life itself. The methods of formulation and the purpose of the rules are determined by class and by the demands of our struggle.

For example, the Revolution threw out into the street the uncouth speech of millions, the slang of the suburbs flowed along central thoroughfares; the enfeebled language of the intelligentsia with its emasculated words: "ideal," "principles of justice," "divine origin," "transcendental image of Christ and Anti-Christ"—all of these whispered restaurant conversations—have been trampled. This is the new element of language. How can it be made poetic? The old rules with their "moons and Junes" and their alexandrines won't do. But how can one introduce everyday speech into poetry and how can one eliminate poetry from everyday speech?

Should one damn the Revolution for the sake of iambs?

> We've become evil and reconciled,
> We can't get away.
> The Railway Board has already separated

The tracks with its black hands.

(Z. Gippius)

No!

It's a hopeless task to try to pack the explosive thunder of the Revolution into a four-foot amphibrach designed for whispering!

> Heroes, wanderers of the oceans, albatrosses,
> Table guests at thunderous banquets,
> Tribe of eagles, sailors and sailors,
> To you a fiery song of ruby words.

(Kirillov)

No!

Let's give all the rights of citizenship to the new language immediately: to a shout instead of a melody, to a thundering drum instead of a lullaby:

> Keep the revolutionary step!
> (Blok)

> Deploy on the march!
> (Mayakovsky)

It is not enough to give examples of the new verse, of rules for acting upon revolutionary crowds by the use of words—it is necessary that this action should aim at maximum support for one's class.

It is not enough to say that the "untiring enemy is always alert" (Blok). It is necessary to show exactly what the enemy looks like, or at least give an unmistakable impression of him.

It is not enough to deploy on the march. It is necessary to deploy according to all the rules of street fighting, so that the telegraph office, the banks, the ammunition depots fall into the hands of the insurgent workers. Hence:

> Gobble your pineapple,

107

Chew at your grouse,
Your last day is coming, you bourgeois louse...

(Mayakovsky)

It is hardly likely that this sort of verse would have been acceptable in classical poetry. Writing in 1820, Grech knew nothing about *chastushki*, but even if he had, he would probably have written about them in the same vein that he wrote about folk verse—that is, scornfully: "These verses know neither meter nor harmony."

Yet the streets of Petersburg have taken these lines to heart. The critics can try to discover at their leisure the basic rules according to which all this was done.

Novelty is obligatory in a poetic work. The material of words and word-combinations which the poet comes across must be re-worked. If, for the making of verse, old scraps of words are used, they must be in strict correlation with the quantity of new material. Whether or not this alloy is fit for use will depend on the quantity and quality of this new element.

Novelty in no way presupposes the constant uttering of unprecedented truths. Iambs, free verse, alliteration, assonance are not created every day. It is also possible to work at extending, deepening, and widening their usage.

"Two twos are four" does not exist on its own and cannot do so. We must know how to apply this fact (rules of application). We must make this fact easy to remember (rules again), and we must show its infallibility in a number of cases (example, content, theme).

It is clear from this that description, the representation of reality, has no independent place in poetry. This kind of work is needed but it should be rated on a par with the work of the secretary of a vast assembly. It is the simple "proposal put—decision taken." In this lies the tragedy of the fellow-travellers: it not only takes them five years to become aware of the proposal, but their decision is also rather belated—after all, the others have carried it out!

Poetry begins with tendentiousness.

In my opinion the poem "I go out alone into the road..." is an incitement to get girls to walk with poets. It's dull on one's own, you see. Oh, if only such a powerful poem were to be written urging people to combine in cooperatives!

The old manuals for writing verse were definitely nothing of the kind. They were only descriptions of historical, traditional ways of writing. The correct title for these books should not be "How to write," but "How they used to write."

I'll be honest about it. I know neither iambs nor trochees, I never could make them out and never will. Not because it is a difficult task, but because in my poetic work I never had anything to do with things like that. And even if bits of such meters did crop up, they were simply something heard and written down, because these tedious rhythms recur much too often—like: "Down the mother-river Volga."

Many a time I took up the study of these things, understood the mechanics of them, and then forgot them. Such things, which take up ninety percent of the poetry manuals, take up less than three percent of my practical work!

In practice, there are only a few general rules for beginning a work of poetry. And even so those rules are pure convention. As in chess. The first moves are almost monotonous. But with the next move one is already beginning to plan a new attack. The most brilliant move cannot be repeated in any given situation in the next game. It is the unexpected move that confounds an opponent.

Just like the unexpected rhymes in verse.

What then are the fundamental requirements for beginning poetic labor?

First. The presence in society of a problem which can only conceivably be solved through a work of poetry. A social command. (An interesting theme for a special work would be—the disparity between a social command and an actual commission.)

Second. An exact knowledge of, or more precisely, an exact sense of the wishes of one's class (or the group one represents) in this matter, that is, pragmatic orientation.

Third. Material. Words. The constant restocking of the storehouses, the granaries of your mind, with all kinds of words, necessary, expressive, rare, invented, renovated, manufactured, and others.

Fourth. Equipment. The business equipment and tools of the trade. Pen, pencil, typewriter, telephone, a suit for visits to the doss-house, a bicycle for riding to editorial offices, a well-arranged table, an umbrella to write under in the rain, living space which allows the particular number of strides necessary to one's work, a connection with a clipping agency to send you information about matters causing concern in the provinces, and so on and so forth, and even a pipe and cigarettes.

Fifth. The skills and methods for processing words, infinitely personal, achieved only after years of daily toil: rhymes, meters, alliterations, images, an inelegant style, pathos, endings, titles, outlines, etc. etc.

For example: social task—providing words for songs of the Red Army men going to the Petersburg front. Pragmatic orientation—to defeat Yudenich. Material—words from the soldiers' vocabulary. Tools of the trade—a chewed-up pencil stump. Method—rhymed chastushka.

Result:

My lass gave me a long felt cloak
and a pair of socks of woolen twine.
Yudenich bolts from Petersburg,
like he was oiled with turpentine.

The novelty of these four lines, which justifies the making of this chastushka, is in the rhyming of "woolen twine" and "turpentine." This novelty makes it relevant, poetic and a model of its genre.

For its impact, the chastushka needs the device of rhyme involving total disparity between the first two lines and the second two. Moreover, the first two lines can be called subsidiary.

Even these general elementary rules for poetic labor will provide more possibilities than there are now for evaluating and describing poetic works.

Features of the material, of the equipment, and of the method can be directly taken into account.

Is there a social command? Yes. Two units. Pragmatic orientation? Two units. Is it rhymed? One more unit. Alliteration? Another half a unit. And for rhythm—one unit, because the peculiar meter required journeys by bus.

Critics may smile, but I would rate the verse of an Alaskan poet (given the same ability, of course) higher than, say, the verse of a man from Yalta.

Indeed I would! The Alaskan has to freeze and spend money on buying a fur coat and the ink in his fountain pen keeps freezing. Whereas the Yalta man writes against a background of palm trees in a spot which is pleasant even without verse.

The same clarity is also introduced into the description of works.

Demyan Bedny's verse represents a correctly understood social command for today, a precise pragmatic orientation—the needs of the workers and peasants—a vocabulary of semi-peasant usage (with an admixture of obsolescent poetic rhymes), and the device of the fable.

The verse of Kruchenykh: alliteration, dissonance, pragmatic orientation—helping future poets.

Here there is no need to concern ourselves with the metaphysical question as to who is better: Demyan Bedny or Kruchenykh. These are poetic works made from different components, on different levels, and each of them can exist without supplanting the other and without competing.

From my point of view, the best poetic work will be that which is written according to the social command of the Comintern, with its aim—the victory of the proletariat—communicated in a new vocabulary, expressive and comprehensible to everyone, made on a table equipped by N.O.T. and delivered to the publishing office by airplane. I insist—by airplane, since the poet's way of life is also one of the most important factors of our industry. Of course, the process of accounting and discounting in poetry is considerably more delicate and complicated than I have shown.

I deliberately emphasize, simplify and caricature my ideas. I emphasize them in order to highlight more sharply the fact that the essence of contemporary works on literature lies not in the evaluation of certain ready-made works from the point of view of taste, but in a correct approach towards the study of the productive process itself.

The present article is not a discussion about ready-made models or methods, but an attempt to reveal the very process of poetic production.

How, then, is verse made?

Work begins long before one receives and becomes aware of the social command.

Preliminary work goes on continuously.

A good poetic work can be made to a deadline only if one has a large reserve of ready poetic stock. Now, for example (I am only writing about what occurs to me at the moment), a good surname, "Mr. Gliceron," derived accidentally from some garbled talk about glycerine, throbs in my brain.

There are also good rhymes:

> (And in the sky the color of) *cream*
> (Arose the austere) *Kremlin*
> (God to Rome, to the French) *to the Germans,*
> (There seek shelter for) *Bohemians.*
> (To the sound of the horse's) *snort*
> (One day I'll ride all the way to) *New York.*
> *New York's*
> *A morgue.*

Or:

> (Rich and) *raucous*
> (Are the days and nights) *of August*

I also like the meter of a certain American song, still requiring alteration and Russification:

> Heard-hearted Hannah
> The vamp of Savannah
> The vamp of Savannah
> Gee-ay.

There are also well-tailored alliterations suggested by the surname "Nita Jo" glimpsed on a poster:

> Where's the joint of Nita Jo?
> Nita's joint is just below.

Or in connection with the dye-works of Lyamina:

> Mummy's job needs lots of stamina—
> Mummy's name is Mrs. Lyamina.

There are themes of varying clarity and obscurity:
(1) Rain in New York.
(2) A prostitute on the Boulevard des Capucines in Paris. A prostitute with whom it is particularly smart to go to bed because she is one-legged—the other having been cut off, it seems, by a tram.
(3) An old male attendant at the lavatory in a huge Hessler restaurant in Berlin.
(4) The vast theme of the October Revolution, which one cannot complete without spending some time in the country, etc., etc.

All these items of poetic stock are stored in my mind. The particularly difficult ones are written down.

How they are to be used in the future I don't know, but I do know that everything will be used.

All my time goes on this storing. I spend between ten and eighteen hours a day on it, and keep muttering something almost incessantly. Concentration on this explains the proverbial absentmindedness of poets.

For me this labor of storing is done with such intensity that in ninety cases out of a hundred I even know the place where, during my fifteen years of work, certain rhymes or alliterations, images, etc., came to me and took final shape.

Astride.

Ride as... (On the tram-ride from Sukhareva Tower to Sretensky Gates, 1913).

The sullen rain screwed up its eye,

It sighed... (Strastnoy Monastery, 1912).

Caress the wasted soot-black cats. (The oak in Kuntsevo, 1914).

Bereft.

Left. (In a cab on the Embankment, 1917).

Son of a bitch, d'Anthès. (On a train near Mytishchi, 1924).

Etc., etc.

This "notebook" is one of the main requirements for the making of an AUTHENTIC work.

People usually write about this notebook only after the death of the writer; for years it lies about amongst rubbish, it gets printed posthumously and after "the finished works"; but for the writer this book is everything.

Naturally, beginners have no such book, just as they have no practice and experience. MANUFACTURED lines are rare, and therefore their poems are thin and long-winded.

Whatever his abilities, a beginner cannot write an impressive work straight away; on the other hand, the first work is always "fresher" because it embodies the poetic stock from the whole of his past life.

It is only the presence of well thought out poetic stock that enables me to finish a work, because when I work hard my normal production is eight to ten lines per day.

Whatever the circumstances, a poet values each meeting, each signboard, each event solely as material to be formed into words.

I used to get so stuck into this work that I was even afraid to utter words and expressions which seemed to me likely to be needed for future verse; I used to become sullen, boring and taciturn.

About 1913, returning from Saratov to Moscow, I said to a woman traveling in the same carriage, in order to prove my respectability, that I was "not a man, but a cloud in trousers." Having said this, I realized at once that it might come in handy for a poem and what if it were spread by word of mouth and wasted to no purpose? Terribly anxious, I spent half an hour plying the girl with leading questions and was only reassured when I satisfied myself that my words had gone in one ear and out the other.

Two years later "a cloud in trousers" came in handy as the title for a whole long poem.

I spent two days thinking about words for the tenderness of a lonely man towards his only love.

How would he cherish and love her?

On the third night I went to bed with a headache, not having thought of anything. In the night the definition came:

> Your body
> I shall cherish and love,
> as a soldier maimed by war,
> un-needed, nobody's,
> cherishes
> his one remaining leg.

I jumped up, half awake. In the dark I wrote down "one remaining leg" on a cigarette pack, using a burned match, and I went back to sleep. In the morning I spent two hours wondering what this "one remaining leg" jotted on the cigarette pack meant and how it could have gotten there.

A rhyme which can almost, but not quite, be pinned down poisons one's existence: you talk without understanding, you eat without appetite and you cannot sleep, almost seeing the rhyme floating before your eyes.

Following the trend started by Shengeli, we began to treat the labor of the poet as a mere trifle. There are even smart lads who have improved on the professor. Here, for example, is one of the advertisements from the Kharkov "Proletarian" (No. 256):

"How to become a writer.
For details send 50 kopeks in stamps to Slavyansk Station, Donetz Railway, P. O. Box No. 11."

How do you like that!

However, this is a pre-revolutionary product. Already, as a supplement to the periodical *Entertainment* a booklet has been sent out, and it's called "How to Become a Poet in Five Lessons."

I think that even my small examples place poetry among the most difficult tasks, which indeed it is.

One's attitude to a line should be like one's attitude to a woman—as in Pasternak's brilliant quatrain:

That day, like some provincial actor
with a Shakespearean play, I roamed the town
lugging you with me, rehearsing you
and I knew you by heart from combs to toes.

In the next chapter I shall try to show the development of these preliminary requirements for making verse, using the writing of one of my own poems as a concrete example.

2

My most effective piece of recent verse is, I think, "To Sergei Esenin."

For this poem there was no need to look for either a magazine or an editor—it was copied by hand before it was printed, it was secretly sneaked out of the composing room and printed in a provincial paper; the audience itself demanded to hear it, and while it was being read you could have heard a pin drop; after the reading people shook my paws, they raved in the corridors and praised it to the skies; and on the day of its publication a review appeared consisting at once of curses and compliments.

How was this poem worked out?

I had known Esenin for a long time—about ten or twelve years.

When I met him for the first time he was wearing bast shoes and a peasant's shirt with some kind of cross-stitch embroidery. The meeting took place in one of the better apartments in Leningrad. Knowing how gladly a real, as opposed to a stage, peasant, changes his garb for shoes and jacket, I did not trust Esenin. He appeared to me theatrical, like a character from an operetta. Even more so because he was already writing appealing verse and clearly could have found the money to buy a pair of boots.

As a man who, in his time, had worn and discarded the yellow blouse, I inquired in a businesslike manner about his clothes.

—What's this? Publicity?

Esenin answered me in a voice like icon-lamp oil brought to life.

Something like:

—We're village folk...we don't understand these ways of yours...we get by somehow...in our homemade old things...

His very capable and very rustic verse was inimical, of course, to us Futurists.

But he was still a funny and endearing fellow.

On leaving I said to him in passing:

—I bet you'll soon drop all these bast shoes and this folksy embroidery!

Esenin objected with passionate conviction. Klyuev led him aside, like a mother leading away a daughter whose virtue is endangered because she fears the girl won't have the strength or will to resist.

I caught sight of Esenin now and then, but it was only after the Revolution that we came face to face at Gorky's house.

With all my innate tactlessness I yelled at him at once:
—Pay up, Esenin, you're wearing a jacket and tie!
Esenin got mad and started to pick a quarrel.
Later I began to come across lines and poems by him which one couldn't help but like, such as:

> My dear, dear funny fool... etc.
> The sky a bell, the moon its tongue...

And others.

Esenin was freeing himself from his idealized rusticity, but not, of course, without lapses, and side by side with: "My mother is my Motherland,/ A Bolshevik is what I am..." there appeared an apologia for "a cow." Instead of a "monument to Marx" there was a compulsive need for a monument to a cow. Not to a dairy cow, but to a symbolic cow, a cow thrusting its horns against a railway engine.

We often had rows with Esenin, blaming him mainly for the Imagism which grew around him like dank undergrowth.

Then Esenin left for America and other places, returning with a marked enthusiasm for things new.

Unfortunately during this period we came across him more often in police records than in poetry. Quickly and surely he was breaking away from the ranks of healthy workers in poetry (I speak of the minimum which is demanded of a poet).

At this time I met Esenin on several occasions, our meetings were elegiac and without the slightest disagreement.

I watched with pleasure Esenin's evolution from Imagism to VAPP. He spoke with interest of other people's verse. There was a new side to the conceited element in Esenin; he felt a certain envy toward all the poets organically welded to the Revolution and to the workers, who saw a great and optimistic road ahead.

This is, I think, the root of Esenin's poetic touchiness, and his self-dissatisfaction, while his excessive drinking and the harsh and clumsy attitudes of those around him did not help matters.

Toward the end Esenin even showed some obvious sympathy

for us (members of LEF): he called on Aseev, rang me up at times, and contrived to run into us.

He became a little soft and flabby but remained elegant in his own Esenin way.

Our last meeting made a painful and profound impression on me. At the cashier's desk of the State Publishing House I met a man who rushed towards me, his face swollen, his tie askew, his hat precariously held in place by a lock of fair hair. He and his two sinister companions (at least from my point of view) reeked of alcohol. I literally had difficulty recognizing Esenin. With difficulty I evaded his immediate desire to drink, which he reinforced by waving a thick wad of ten-ruble notes. All day I kept recalling how he looked sick, and that evening I argued with my friends at length that something should be done about him (unfortunately, such matters never go beyond this). Both they and I blamed his "milieu," and we parted convinced that Esenin was being cared for by his friends—the Esenin crowd.

It turned out differently. Esenin's end saddened us with the sadness common to all humanity. But this end immediately appeared completely natural and logical. I heard about it in the night, and my sadness would have probably remained sadness and abated towards morning, had not the morning papers carried his last lines:

> In this life there's nothing new in dying,
> But in living there is nothing newer.

After these lines Esenin's death became a fact of literature.

It immediately became clear how many unstable people this powerful poem, precisely a poem, VERSE, would bring to the noose and the revolver.

And no newspaper analyses or articles could ever erase this poem.

One can and should counter this poem with a poem, and NOTHING BUT A POEM, verse.

Thus the poets of the U.S.S.R. were given a social command

119

to write verse about Esenin. An exceptional command, important and urgent, because Esenin's lines began to take effect quickly and unerringly. Many accepted the command. But write what? How?

There appeared verse, articles, reminiscences, literary sketches, and even plays. In my opinion ninety-nine percent of what was written about Esenin was either simply claptrap, or else damaging claptrap.

The verses written by Esenin's friends are trivial. You can always recognize them by the way they address Esenin familiarly as "Seryozha" (this is where Bezymensky found this unsuitable word). "Seryozha" as a literary fact does not exist. There is a poet—Sergei Esenin. And as such we ask you to speak of him. Introducing the familiar "Seryozha" immediately disrupts the social command and overall design. The word "Seryozha" reduces a grave and important theme to the level of an epigram or a lyric. And no amount of weeping by his poetic kinsmen will help. Poetically these verses cannot impress. They provoke laughter and irritation.

Although Esenin's "enemies" were placated by his death, their verses are pious humbug. They simply refuse him a poetic burial because of the very fact of his suicide.

> We never thought that even you could be
> Such a wicked hooligan as this... *(Zharov,* I think).

These are the verses of those who hastily fulfill a poorly understood social command, the pragmatic orientation of which is entirely unconnected with the method, and of those who adopt a feuilleton style which is totally ineffective in this tragic instance.

Torn out of its complicated social and psychological circumstances, Esenin's suicide with its unmotivated moment of negation (what else could it be?!) is depressing in its falsity.

The prose written about Esenin is of little help in fighting against the harmfulness of his last poem.

120

Let's start with Kogan, who in my opinion tried to deduce Marxism on his own, not from studying Marx, but from Luka's dictum: "Fleas are not so bad, they are all black and they all jump," which truth he considers the height of scientific objectivity, and who, therefore, in Esenin's absence (after his death) wrote a laudatory article now no longer needed; and let's end with the stinking little books by Kruchenykh, who instructs Esenin in elementary political theory, as though Kruchenykh himself had spent all his life in a forced labor camp suffering for freedom and as though it were a great effort for him to write six (!) booklets about Esenin with a hand still bearing the marks of jangling fetters.

So what and how should one write about Esenin? Having examined his death from all points of view and delved into other people's material, I formulated and set myself the problem.

Pragmatic orientation: deliberately to neutralize the effect of Esenin's last poem, to make his end uninteresting, to replace the bland beauty of death with another kind of beauty—because working humanity needs all its strength for the Revolution which has started, and because in spite of the hardship of the road and the painful contradictions of the NEP, it demands that we glorify the joy of life, the happiness of the immensely difficult march to communism.

Now that I have the poem in front of me, these things are easy to formulate, but how hard it was when I started writing.

The work coincided with my travels in the provinces where I was giving lectures. For about three months I kept returning to the theme, day in, day out, but I could not think up anything worthwhile. All kinds of evil nonsense teeming with water-pipes and livid faces crowded into my mind. In three months I hadn't come up with a single line. From the daily sifting of words some stock rhymes emerged, such as "in some — hansom," "Kogan — blowgun," "Napostov — boast of." When I was already on my way back to Moscow I realized that the slowness and difficulty of the writing was due to the excessive similarity between what I was describing and my personal environment.

The same hotel rooms, the same water-pipes, the same enforced solitude.

This environment wrapped itself around me, did not let me escape, did not yield either sensations or the words needed to damn and deny, and did not provide me with the essentials for evoking optimism.

From this one can almost draw a rule: to make a poetic work, a change of place or time is essential.

Just as, for example, in painting, when sketching an object one must walk back to a distance equal to three times its size. Unless you do this you simply will not be able to see the object you are depicting.

The bigger the object or event, the greater the distance you will have to walk away. The feeble cool their heels, waiting for an event to pass them by so that they can reflect it, the powerful run just far enough ahead to give the pull to the times, which they have understood.

The description of contemporary events by those taking part in the struggles of the day will always be incomplete, even incorrect, at any rate—one-sided.

It is obvious that such labor is the sum, the result of two kinds of work—the records of a contemporary, and the generalizing labor of tomorrow's artist. This is the tragedy of the revolutionary writer: he can present a brilliant report, for example *The Week* by Libedinsky, and yet be hopelessly wrong in drawing general conclusions without perspective. If not the perspective of time and place, at least mental perspective.

Thus, for instance, deference to "poetry" at the expense of facts and news reports prompted the workers' correspondents to issue the collection *Petals* with verse like:

> I am a proletarian gun,
> I fire about come rain or sun.

There is a lesson in this: (1) let's drop the delirious ramblings about unfurling "epic canvasses" while fighting on the barricades—all the canvasses will be torn to shreds, (2) the value of factual material (hence the interest in the reports of the workers' rural correspondents) at the time of a revolution should be rated higher, or at least no lower, than a so-called "poetic work." Premature poeticization only emasculates and distorts the material. All handbooks of poetry à la Shengeli are harmful because they do not elicit the poetry from the material, that is, do not give the essence of facts, do not compress facts to the point where the result becomes a concentrated, compact economical word, but merely dress up new facts in any old form. More often than not, the form is the wrong size: either the fact is completely lost like a flea in a pair of trousers, as, for example, Radimov's piglets get lost in his Greek pentameters, better suited to the *Iliad,* or—the fact sticks out from the poetic clothing and becomes ridiculous instead of sublime. That's how, for example, "The Sailors" look in Kirillov's poem, walking in procession in his worn-out, overstuffed, amphibracic tetrameters.

A change of surroundings, away from the one where this or that fact took place, a certain distance, is essential.

This does not mean, of course, that a poet should sit by the sea waiting for good weather, while time goes by. He must urge time onward. He must substitute a change of place for the slow passage of time, and, in his imagination, must let a century pass in the space of a day.

For slight, short pieces this substitution can and should be made artificially (and in fact this happens of itself).

It is good to begin writing a poem about the First of May in November or December, when the desire for May is desperately strong.

In order to write about gentle love take the No. 7 bus from Lubyanskaya Square to Nogin Square. The terrible jolting is the best way of making you appreciate, by contrast, the charm of another kind of life. Jolting is essential for comparison.

Time is also needed to perfect already written works.

All of the poetry I wrote in the white heat of inspiration on topical themes pleased me when I was writing it. Nevertheless, a day later it seemed petty, unfinished, one-sided. I always wanted terribly to alter something.

That's why, when I have completed a work, I lock it up in my writing desk for a few days, after which I take it out and see at once the defects that were not previously apparent.

I'd been overdoing it.

This does not necessarily mean that one should write only non-topical works. No. Quite the contrary—they should be topical. I am merely focussing the attention of poets on the fact that rhymed propaganda slogans, which are considered easy, in reality demand the most intensive effort and the most varied devices to make up for the lack of time.

Even when preparing an urgent piece of propaganda one should, for instance, make a revised copy in the evening and not in the morning. In the morning one can see at a glance many things which can easily be corrected. But if one makes a revised copy in the morning most of what is bad will be left there. The know-how for creating distances and organizing time (but not the iambs and the trochees) must be included as a basic rule in every effective handbook of poetry.

That is why during the short drive from Lubyansky Passage to the Tea Marketing Boards in Myasnitskaya Street (on my way to redeem an advance payment) I was able to do more of my poem about Esenin than during the whole of my journey. Myasnitskaya Street was a sharp and necessary contrast: after the solitude of hotel rooms—the crowded Myasnitskaya Street; after the provincial quietude—the excitement and liveliness of the buses, cars and trams; and all around, as a challenge to the old rush-lit villages—the electrified engineering offices.

I walk about, gesticulating, mumbling still almost without words, now shortening my steps in order not to impede my mumbling, now mumbling more quickly in time to my steps.

Thus is the rhythm hewn and shaped—the rhythm which is the basis of all poetic work and which goes through it like a rumble. Gradually from this rumbling one begins to squeeze out single words.

Some words simply rebound and never return, others linger, turn over, and twist themselves inside out several dozen times until one feels that the word has fallen into place. (This feeling, developed through experience, is called talent.) First and most frequently, the main word becomes apparent—the main word which characterizes the meaning of the verse or the word which is to be rhymed. The remaining words come and arrange themselves in relation to the main one. When the fundamentals are done there suddenly emerges a sensation that the rhythm has been violated—some tiny syllable or small sound is lacking. One begins to tailor all the words anew and this work drives one to distraction. It is as though for the hundredth time a crown is being unsuccessfully fitted to a tooth, and finally, after the hundredth attempt, is it pressed and falls into place. The similarity for me is strengthened, morever, by the fact that when, finally, that crown "falls into place" tears gush from my eyes (literally)— from pain and from a sense of relief.

It is not clear where that basic "rumble-rhythm" comes from. To me it is any repetition within me of a sound, noise or slight rocking, or even, generally speaking, the repetition of any phenomenon which I connect with sound. The repetitive surge of the sea; the maid who slams the door each morning and, repeating herself, plods along, shuffling in the back of my mind; and even the revolving of the earth which, for me, seems inevitably connected, in a funny way, with the repeated turning of a globe in a shop for visual aids in the whistling of a rising wind.

The endeavor to organize movement, to organize sounds around oneself, discovering their nature, their peculiarities, is one of the main, unceasing poetic tasks—the stockpiling of rhythms. I don't know whether rhythm exists outside me or only within me, most   likely—within me. But to awaken it there has to be a jolt: thus some unknown creaking noise starts a rumbling in the belly of a grand piano, thus too a bridge begins to rock, threatening to collapse from the synchonized steps of many ants.

Rhythm is the basic force, the basic energy of verse. It is

impossible to explain it, one can only talk about it as one talks about magnetism or electricity. Magnetism and electricity are forms of energy. There can be a single rhythm in many verses, even throughout the whole work of a poet, and this does not make the work tedious because rhythm can be so complicated and difficult that one cannot get at it even with the aid of several long poems.

The poet must develop in himself precisely this feeling of rhythm and not memorize other people's rhythms: iambs, trochees, or even the canonized free verse—all are rhythms adapted for some precise occasion and fitted exclusively for this precise occasion. Thus, for instance, the magnetic energy given to a horseshoe will attract steel filings and cannot be used for any other purpose.

As to meters, I don't know any of them. For myself, I am simply convinced that for heroic or majestic assignments one should use long meters with a large number of syllables, and for light-hearted ones—short meters. For some reason, ever since my childhood (from the age of about nine) all the former kind have been associated in my mind with: "Victims you fell in the terrible fight..." and the latter with: "We'll defeat the decadent order..."

Curious. But I give you my word it is so.

In my case meter is arrived at as a result of overlaying this rhythmic rumble with words, words prompted by the aim and orientation one has in mind (one keeps asking oneself: is this the right word? to whom shall I read this? will it be understood correctly? etc.), words controlled by the highest degree of sensitivity, abilities and talent.

To begin with, the poem to Esenin started as a kind of rumbling which went something like this:

Da-da-dá/ da dá/ da, da da, dá/ da dá/
da-da-di/ da da da/ da da/ da da da da/
da-da-da/ da-da da da da dadi
da-da-da/ da da-da/ dada/ da/ da da

Later words emerged:

> You have gone da da da da da another world.
> It may be you fly da da da da da.
> Neither advance for you, nor skirt, nor pub.
> Da da da/ da da da da/ sobriety.

I kept repeating this dozens of times, listening carefully to the first line: "You have gone da da da to another world," etc. What is this damned "da da da" and what can replace it? Perhaps I should leave out the "dadada" altogether.

> You have gone to another world.

No! Some verse I had heard before immediately comes to mind:

> The steed fell on the battlefield.

Who wants a steed! We are not talking of horses but of Esenin. And even without these syllables some kind of operatic gallop is arrived at, whereas this "da da da" is much more exalted. One cannot drop this "da da da" at any cost –the rhythm is correct. I begin to try out words.

> You have gone, Seryozha, to another world...
> You have gone beyond return to another world.
> You have gone, Esenin, to another world.

Which of these lines is best?
All rubbish! Why?
The first line is false because of the word "Seryozha." I never addressed Esenin in this grossly familiar way, and this word is inadmissible even now, since it brings in its wake a lot of other false words foreign to me and uncharacteristic of our relationship such as: "thou," "gentle," "brother" etc.

127

The second line is bad because the words "beyond return" are not inevitable but accidental, put in only for the sake of meter: they not only fail to help, and explain nothing, but they just get in the way. Indeed, what does "beyond return" mean? Has anyone ever died not beyond return? Is there a death with a return ticket?

The third line is no good because of its utter seriousness (the orientation I had in mind gradually drums it into my head that this is the failing of all three lines). Why is this seriousness unacceptable? Because it permits people to ascribe to me a biblical-sounding belief, which I do not hold, in the existence of an afterlife. This is one reason, and another is that this seriousness makes the verse simply funereal instead of tendentious and it obscures the pragmatic orientation. This is why I introduce the words "as people say."

"You have gone, as people say, to another world." The line is done; "as people say," while not directly mocking, subtly reduces the pathetic element of the verse and simultaneously removes any suspicion about the author believing in some beyond-the-grave nonsense. The line is done, and at once becomes the basic one, determining the whole of the quatrain, which must be made to serve a dual purpose, neither breaking into dance on the sorrowful occasion nor, on the other hand, indulging in a tearful whine. The quatrain must be split in half straightaway: two solemn lines and two colloquial, popular lines, each set enhancing the other by contrast. That's why, because of my conviction that for light-hearted lines one should have fewer syllables, I immediately tackle the ending of the quatrain:

> Neither advance for you, nor skirt, nor pub,
> da da dá da da dá da dá sobriety.

What shall I do with these lines? How shall I cut them down? The words "nor skirt" must be taken out. Why? Because these "skirts" are living people. It is tactless to call them this when the greater part of Esenin's lyrical verse is dedicated to them with great tenderness. And that's why it is false, that's why it lacks resonance. What remains then—"Neither advance for you, nor pub."

I attempt to mutter it to myself—it doesn't work. These lines are so different from the first ones that the rhythm does not change, it simply breaks and tears. I have cut out too much. What then is to be done? Some absurd syllable is missing. This line, in breaking away from the rhythm, has become false. It is false from another point of view, too—that of its meaning. There is insufficient contrast and, moreover, it blames Esenin alone for all the "advances and pubs," whereas they apply equally to all of us.

How then can I make these lines even more contrasting and at the same time more generalized?

I take the most common saying:

> —There's no floor for you, nor roof—
>
> —There's no advance for you, nor pub.

In the most colloquial, the must vulgar form they say:

> —no floor for you, no roof—
>
> —no advance for you, no pub.

The line fell into place as regards meter and meaning. The familiar mode of address "for you" [in Russian *tebe*] is in even greater contrast to the formal mode of address in the first lines of the poem. The formal address in the first line, "You have gone.." [in Russian, *Vy ushli*] and the familiar form "for you" [*tebe*] in the third line at once show that advance payments and pubs are not brought in to degrade the memory of Esenin, but as a general phenomenon. This line turned out to be a good point of departure for discarding all the syllables before "sobriety," and this sobriety itself turned out to be something like a solution to the problem. Therefore the quatrain attracts the sympathy of even the keenest supporters of Esenin, while remaining essentially almost a sneer.

The quatrain is basically ready, with only one line still left to be filled in with rhyme.

You have gone, as people say, to another world,
it may be you fly da-da-dá-da.
No advance for you, no pub –
sobriety.

Perhaps one could leave it unrhymed? No. Why? Because without rhyme (meaning rhyme in a broad sense) the verse falls to pieces.

The rhyme sends you back to the previous line, makes you remember it, makes all the lines shaping one thought hold together.

A rhyme is usually defined as a consonance of the last words in two lines when the same stressed vowel and the sounds following it approximately coincide.

Everybody says this, but all the same it is rubbish.

Consonance at the end of lines, rhyme, is only one of the innumerable ways of tying lines together and, by the way, the simplest and crudest.

It is also possible to rhyme the beginnings of lines:

astride—
ride as the grand land owner... etc.

One can rhyme the end of a line with the beginning of the next line:

the sullen rain screwed up its eye,
it sighed, the while behind... etc.

It is possible to take the ending of the first and second lines and make the final word of the third or fourth line rhyme with both of them at once:

from a scholarly angle
barely
could Russian verse be made out by Shengeli

130

etc., etc., ad infinitum.

In my quatrain it is necessary to rhyme the word "sobriety." The first words that come into my head could be words such as "impropriety," for example:

> You have gone, as people say, to another world,
> it may be you fly... I know your impropriety!
> No advance for you, no pub—
> sobriety.

Can one leave this rhyme as it is? No. Why? First of all because this rhyme is too exact, too transparent. When you say "impropriety" the rhyme "sobriety" thrusts itself forward and when uttered it does not surprise nor arrest one's attention. This is the fate of almost all cognate words, if a verb is rhymed with a verb, a noun with a noun, when they have the same roots or cases, etc. The word "impropriety" is also wrong because, even in the first lines, it introduces the element of derision, and in this way it weakens all subsequent contrasts. Perhaps it would be possible to make one's task easier by replacing the word "sobriety" by some word which rhymes more easily or not to place "sobriety" at the end of the line but to fill out the line with several syllables, for example, "sobriety, stillness"?... In my opinion this should not be done; I always place the most characteristic word at the end of a line and find a rhyme for it at all costs. As a result my rhyming is almost always unusual, or at any rate my rhymes have not been used before and are not in the rhyming dictionary.

Rhyme ties lines together, therefore its fabric should be even stronger than the fabric used for the remaining lines.

Taking the most distinctive sound—"briet"—of the word "sobriety" which is being rhymed, I repeat it lots of times to myself, listening carefully to all its associations: "briet," "bright," "brighter," "rioter," "rightly," "vitally," "mightily." An apt rhyme has been found. An adverb, and moreover, a solemn one!

But there's the rub: in the word "sobriety" the sounds

"s" and "t" can be heard. What can be done with them? It is necessary to introduce analagous letters in the previous line too.

That's why the words "it may be" are replaced by the word "emptiness" with its "t" and "s's" and we keep the word "fly" which, with its soft "l" sound offsets the sound of the "t."

And here is the final version:

> You have gone, as people say, to another world.
> Emptiness,—you fly, sundering the stars mightily...
> No advance for you, no pub —
> sobriety.

It is self-evident that I am over-simplifying, schematizing and subjecting poetic labor to a selective mental process. Obviously, the process of writing is more circuitous, more intuitive. But all the same the labor, basically, follows a scheme like this.

The first quatrain defines all the subsequent poem. Now that I have this quatrain before me I can estimate how many of them will be needed for the given theme, and how to distribute them to the best effect: the architectonics of poetry.

The theme is big and complex: as well as quatrains it will be necessary to use six-line stanzas and two-line stanzas—in all about twenty to thirty bricks.

After manufacturing almost all these bricks, I start trying them for size, fitting them now in one place, now in another, listening carefully to the way they sound and trying to imagine the impression they create.

Having done some of this fitting, and having thought it through, I make the following decision: to begin with, I must capture the interest of every listener by means of ambiguity, so that it is not clear whose side I am on, then I must take Esenin away from those who exploit his death for their own profit, I must praise him and exonerate him as his admirers "driving their flat rhymes into the mound" failed to do. One must finally win the sympathy of the listeners by heavily coming down on all those Sobinovs and Kogans, those who vulgarize Esenin's work—

even more so because they vulgarize any other work they tackle—while carrying the listeners along with what are, by now, easy couplets. After winning over the listeners, and having wrested from them the right to speak about the achievements of Esenin and his group, I must then suddenly direct them towards a conviction of the complete worthlessness, insignificance and unimportance of Esenin's end by rephrasing his own last words, giving them a contrary meaning.

As a simple figure, one comes up with the following diagram:

When you've got the quatrains, the basic building bricks, and when you have devised a general plan of construction, the basic work can be regarded as over.

Next comes the relatively easy technical processing of the poetic work.

The expressiveness of the verse must be taken to its utmost limits. One of the chief ways of making the poem expressive is the use of images. Not the basic image or vision, which arises at the start of the work as an indistinct initial response to the social command. No, I am speaking of the auxiliary images which help the main one to grow. This image is one of the usual devices of poetry, and certain movements such as, for example, Imagism, made it their goal, thereby condemning themselves in essence to developing only one of the technical aspects of poetry.

There are innumerable ways of manufacturing images.

One of the elementary ways of making an image is by the use of comparisons. My first works, for example, *A Cloud in Trousers,* were built entirely on comparisons—always "like, like and like." It is, perhaps, this primitive element which makes later critics consider *A Cloud* the "culmination" of my work. In later works and in my "Esenin" this primitive element is eradicated. I found only one comparison: "tediously and at length like Doronin."

Why like Doronin, and not, say, like the distance to the moon? First of all, the comparison is taken from literary life, since the whole theme is that of a man of letters. And secondly— "The Iron Ploughman" (did I get that right?) is longer than the road to the moon, because the road does not exist, whereas "The Iron Ploughman" unfortunately does; and then again the road to the moon would seem shorter because of its novelty, whereas four thousand lines by Doronin startle one with the monotony of a verbal and rhyme landscape which has already been seen sixteen thousand times. And then, the image itself must be tendentious; that is to say, in developing an important theme, one should, for the sake of the struggle and literary propaganda, exploit all the minor independent images one comes across along the way.

The most widespread method of making an image is that of using a metaphor, i.e., transferring definitions which up to now have belonged only to certain things to other words, things, phenomena, and concepts, as well.

For instance, the metaphor in the line: "And they carry the funeral scrap of verse."

We are familiar with iron scrap, food scraps. But how does one define the poetic trash which has remained unused, left over from poetic works? Of course it is the scrap of verse, verse scrap. Here this scrap is of only one kind—funeral, it is the funeral verse scrap. But this line cannot be left as it stands because it becomes "funeral verse scrap", i.e., "scrap" which can be read "crap" and this so-called SHIFT distorts the whole meaning of the verse. This kind of carelessness occurs very often.

For instance, in the lyrical poem by Utkin, which recently appeared in *Projector,* there are the lines: "He will not come, just as/ The summer swan alights not on winter lakes."

The word "snot" is clearly heard in the second line.

The first line of a poem published by Bryusov in the early days of the war in the magazine *Our Times* is most effective: "We are veterans, our wounds are hurting us." *[Note: Mayakovsky's non-existent comment on this line is hardly necessary here since the sequence of syllables in the Russian makes up the passive participle of the verb "to shit."]*

This shift is disposed of and, at the same time, the order of the words gives the simplest and most clear-cut definition: "the scrap of funeral verse."

One of the methods of making images that I have been using more and more recently is the creation of utterly fantastic events —incidents emphasized by the use of hyperbole:

> So that Kogan should rush away in all directions
> crippling everyone he met with the spears of his
> >   moustaches.

In this way Kogan becomes a collective image which makes it possible for him to rush in all directions, and for his moustaches to turn into spears; and to enhance this "spear-quality," people lie around crippled by his moustaches.

Methods of image construction are varied, as is all the rest of the verse-making technique, depending on the extent to which the reader is surfeited with one or another of the forms.

In addition, there may be imagery of the opposite kind, that is, imagery which, far from mentally extending what has been said, tries on the contrary to condense the impression given by the words into a deliberately limited framework. For example in my old poem *War and the World:*

> In a rotting truck forty men—
> and only four legs.

Many of Selvinsky's works are based on such numerical images.

Next comes the labor of selecting verbal material. It is necessary to take into account with great precision the milieu in which the poetic work develops, so that no word foreign to this milieu gets in by accident.

For example, I had the line: "You had the skill, my friend, to do such things."

"My friend" is false, firstly because it cuts across the severe denunciatory treatment of the work; secondly, we never used this term in our poetic milieu. Thirdly, it is a weak term, habitually used in insignificant conversations, rather more to conceal feeling than to throw it into relief; fourthly, it is natural for a man truly overcome by grief to conceal this with coarser words. Moreover, this term does not define what things the friend had the skill to do—what was it you could do?

What did Esenin have the skill to do? Today there is a great demand for and an intent and admiring focussing on his lyrics; Esenin's literary development moved along the line of so-called literary scandal (not an offensive thing but exceedingly respectable, an echo, a side-effect of the famous public appearances of the Futurists). And it was precisely these scandals which, during his lifetime, were Esenin's literary milestones and stages.

How unsuitable the following would be to the living Esenin: "You had the skill to sing such things to the soul."

Esenin did not sing (in essence he is, of course, the gypsy-guitar type, but his poetic salvation lay in the fact that, at least during his life, he was not taken for such, and that in his volumes there are a dozen or so poetic innovations). Esenin did not sing, he was rude, he used bad language. It was only after long consideration that I put down "bad language," however annoying such a term might be to those brought up in literary brothels, hearing nothing all day but "bad language" while dreaming of unburdening their hearts in poetry about lilacs, bosoms, trilling nightingales, harmonies and tender cheeks. Without any comment I shall now demonstrate how the words in one line were gradually worked out.

1. our times are poorly equipped for gaiety;
2. our times are poorly equipped for joy;
3. our times are poorly equipped for happiness;
4. our life is poorly equipped for gaiety;
5. our life is poorly equipped for joy;
6. our life is poorly equipped for happiness;
7. for merrymaking our planet is poorly equipped;

8. for merriment our planet is poorly equipped;
9. our planet is not specially well equipped for merry-making,
10. our planet is not specially well equipped for gaiety;
11. our puny little planet is not well equipped for pleasures;

and finally, the last, twelfth line:

12. for gaiety our planet is poorly equipped.

I could deliver a whole speech in support of the last of these lines, but for the present I shall simply content myself with copying the lines from my rough notes in order to demonstrate how much labor it takes to produce a few words.

The sound-quality of a poetic work, the linking of word with word, is also included in the technical processing. This "word magic," this "perhaps everything in our life is but a means for brightly singing verse,"—this sound-element also seems to many to be the aim of poetry, which once again reduces poetry to the level of technical labor. If one overdoes alliteration, consonance, and so on, one creates an impression of satiety after a minute's reading.

For example, Balmont: "I'm a wandering wind and I wend to the west weaving a way through the waves," etc.

It is necessary to use doses of alliteration with extreme care and as far as possible without ostentatious repetition. An example of clear alliteration in my Esenin poem is the line: "Where is it, the resounding bronze, the grinding edge of granite..."

I resort to alliteration to frame and underline even more strongly the word which is of importance to me. One can resort to alliteration simply in order to play with words, for poetic amusement; poets of the past (who for us are the old poets) used alliteration mainly for its melodiousness, for its verbal music, and therefore, often used the type of alliteration I most hate—onomatopoeia. I have already spoken about such methods of alliteration in connection with rhyme.

137

Of course, it isn't obligatory to pack one's verse with fancy alliteration and to rhyme it throughout in improbable ways. Always remember that the policy of economy in art is the most important rule for every production of esthetic value. Therefore, when one has completed the basic work, of which I spoke at the beginning, many esthetic passages and fancy bits must be deliberately toned down, so that other passages will gain in brilliance.

It is possible, for example, to half-rhyme lines, to connect a verb which grates on the ear with another verb, in order to lead up to a brilliant thunder-clap of rhyme.

This serves to underline, once again, the relativity of all rules for writing verse.

The technical labor also includes the intonational side of poetic work.

It is impossible to work at a poem which is to function in an airless void, or, as often happens with poetry, in a void that is only too airy.

It is necessary to have constantly before one's eyes the audience to whom the poem is addressed. This is particularly important at the present time when the chief means of contact with the masses is the auditorium, the public platform, the voice, the spoken word.

It is necessary to adapt one's tone to suit the audience—to make it persuasive, pleading, commanding or questioning.

Most of my poems are constructed in a conversational tone. But despite careful consideration this tone is not strictly fixed, but is a method of address which I frequently change during a reading, depending on the composition of the audience. Thus, for example, the printed text says, rather indifferently, counting on a well-qualified reader:

Happiness has to be snatched from the days to come.

Sometimes at public readings I amplify this line to a shout:

Slogan:

snatch your happiness from the days to come!

Therefore, there is no need to be surprised if someone puts out the poem, even in its printed form, with the words arranged to suit several different moods, and with particular expressions for each occasion.

When one has made a poem intended for print, one must take into account how this printed poem will be understood *as* printed poem. It is necessary to take into consideration the ordinariness of the reader, it is necessary in every possible way to make the reader's interpretation approximate the very one which the poet intended to give his poetic line. Our usual punctuation, with its full stops, commas, exclamation marks and question marks, is too poor and inexpressive compared with the shades of emotion which today's more sophisticated man puts into a poetic work.

The meter and rhythm of a poem are more significant than the punctuation, and the punctuation is subordinated to them when it is used in its old form. Nonetheless everyone reads these lines by Alexei Tolstoy:

> Shibanov said nought. From the wound in his foot
> The scarlet blood flowed in a stream...

as:

> Shibanov said nought from the wound in his foot...

And again:

> No more, ashamed I am
> To lower myself before the haughty Pole...

reads like provincial chit-chat:

> No more ashamed I am...

In order that this be read as Pushkin intended it, one must divide the line as I do:

> No more,
>   ashamed I am...

With such a division into half-lines there will be no muddle either as to meaning or as to rhythm. The division of lines is often dictated, moreover, by the necessity of hammering out the rhythm with absolute precision, because our condensed, economical verse structure frequently makes us discard the intervening words and syllables, and if, after these syllables, no pause is made—often a bigger pause than between the lines—the rhythm will snap.

That's why I write:

> Emptiness...
>   You fly,
>   sundering the stars, mightily.

"Emptiness" stands alone, as the sole word characterizing the celestial landscape. "You fly" stands alone to avoid the imperative meaning: "fly sundering," etc.

One of the important features of a poem, particularly a tendentious, declamatory one, is the ending. The most successful lines of the poem are usually put in the ending. Sometimes one has to recast the whole verse solely to justify such an arrangement.

In my poem about Esenin this ending naturally consisted of a re-phrasing of Esenin's last lines.

They sound like this:

Esenin's: In this life there's nothing new in dying,
               But to go on living is no newer.

Mine: In this life there's nothing hard in dying.
               To make one's life have meaning is much harder.

During my extensive work on the whole poem I constantly thought of these lines. While working on other lines I kept returning to these—consciously or unconsciously.

It was utterly impossible to forget that this was the only way to do it; therefore I did not write down these lines but made them in my head (as I previously used to make all my poems, and still make the most striking ones).

That's why it is not possible to reckon the number of versions, but in any case there were no fewer than fifty or sixty variants of these two lines.

The methods by which words are technically processed are infinitely varied, and to talk about them would be pointless since the basis of poetic labor, as I have frequently mentioned here, consists precisely in inventing methods for this processing, and it is exactly these methods which make a writer a professional. The Talmudists of poetry will probably make a wry face over this book of mine because they like to give ready-made poetic recipes. Take a certain theme, clothe it in poetic form, iambs or trochees, rhyme the ends, slip in a dash of alliteration, stuff with images—and the poem is ready.

But in every editorial office they throw this simple handiwork into the wastepaper basket over and over again (and a good thing too).

A man who picks up his pen for the first time and wants to be writing poetry a week later will not need this book.

My book will be of use to the man who, despite all obstacles, wants to be a poet, the man who, knowing that poetry is one of the most difficult productive processes, wants to acquire and hand down certain seemingly mysterious methods of this craft.

Conclusions:

1. Poetry is a productive process. A most difficult, most complicated one, but still a productive process.

2. Training in poetic labor is not a study in the preparation of a definite, limited type of poetic work, but a study of the methods used in any poetic labor and of the productive skills

which help to create new skills.

3. Novelty, novelty of material and of method, is obligatory for every poetic work.

4. The labor of a verse-maker must be practiced daily to improve's one's craftsmanship and to collect one's poetic stock.

5. A good notebook and the ability to use it are more important than the ability to write faultlessly in meters which have kicked the bucket long ago.

6. There is no need to start a vast poetic factory going in order to make poetic cigarette lighters. One should turn one's back on such irrational poetic trivialities. One should take up one's pen only when there is no other way of speaking except in verse. One should produce finished verse only when one feels a clear social command.

7. To understand the social command correctly, the poet should be at the center of things and events. A knowledge of economic theory, a knowledge of the realities of life, a grounding in the study of scientific history, are more important for the poet—in the early stages of his labor—than are the scholastic textbooks of idealist professors who worship old junk.

8. To fulfill the social command most satisfactorily, it is necessary to be in the vanguard of one's class, it is necessary, together with one's class, to struggle on all fronts. The fairy tale about apolitical art must be smashed to smithereens. This ancient fairy tale is now emerging in a new form under cover of idle chatter about "wide epic canvasses" (first—epic, then—objective, and finally—non-Party), about a grand style (first—grand, then elevated, and finally, spiritual) etc., etc.

9. Only by regarding art as a productive process can we eliminate the accidental, the lack of discrimination in taste, and the subjectivity of evaluation. Only this will bring into harmony the various types of literary labor: both verse and the report of the workers' correspondent. Instead of mystical discussions on a poetic theme, this will give us an opportunity for a precise approach to the immediate problem of how to rate and assess poetry.

10. One should not attribute an independent value to workmanship, the so-called technical processing. But it is precisely this workmanship which makes a poetic work fit for use. It is only the difference between the methods of processing that makes the difference between poets, it is only knowledge, a striving for perfection, the accumulation and variation of literary methods, that make a man into a professional writer.

11. The poet's everyday circumstances influence the creation of a real work of art in the same way as all the other factors. The word "Bohemian" has become synonymous with commonplace artistic philistines. Unfortunately, a struggle was waged against the word Bohemian and only against the word. In reality we are faced with the old atmosphere of individualist literary career-mongering, of petty malicious group interests, of mutual intrigue, the notion "poetic" being supplanted by "loose-living," "boozy," "lout," etc. Even the poet's clothes, even his conversations with his wife at home must be different, determined by his entire poetic activity.

12. We, the members of LEF, never say that we are the only possessors of the secrets of poetic creation. But we are the only ones who want to reveal these secrets, the only ones who do not want, for the sake of profit, to surround creativity with artistic-religious worship.

My present attempt is the weak attempt of one man alone, using the theoretical works written by my comrades, the students of literature.

It is necessary for these students of literature to adapt their work to contemporary material and directly help the future development of poetic labor.

But this is not enough.

It is necessary that the authorities for mass education should give the teaching of old esthetic junk a thorough shake-up.

Translated by Valentina Coe

Marina Tsvetaeva

ART IN THE LIGHT OF CONSCIENCE

"Holy art," "art is holy"—however common this common-place, it does have some meaning, and there really *is* one in a thousand who thinks of what he is saying and says just what he is thinking.

To that one in a thousand who consciously affirms the holiness of art I am addressing myself.

What is holiness? Holiness is a condition the reverse of sin, our age does not know sin, our age replaces the concept of sin with the concept of harm. It follows that for an atheist there can be no question of the holiness of art, he will talk of the use of art or the beauty of art. Therefore, I insist, what I say is addressed exclusively to those for whom God—sin—holiness—*are*.

If an atheist speaks of the loftiness of art, then what I say will partly concern him too.

What is art?

Art is the same as nature. Don't seek in it other laws than its own (don't seek the self-will of the artist, which doesn't exist, but precisely—the laws of art). Perhaps art is only a ramification of nature (a species of its creation). The truth is: a product of art is a product of nature, just as much a born, not a made, thing. (And what of all the labor towards its realization? But the earth labors too—in French it's *"la terre en travail."* And isn't birth itself labor? Female gestation and the artist's gestation of his work have been spoken of so often they don't need insisting on: everyone knows—and everyone knows correctly.)

What is the difference then between a product of art and a product of nature, between a poem and a tree? There is none.

145

Whatever paths of labor and wonder lead to it, it *is*. "I am!"

So the artist is the earth giving birth, and giving birth to everything. For the glory of God? What about spiders? (There are some,even among the works of art.)I don't know for whose glory but I think it is a question not of glory but of strength.

Is nature holy? No. Sinful? No. But if a work of art is also a work of nature, why do we expect something of a poem and not of a tree—at most we regret that it grows crooked.

Because the earth giving birth is irresponsible, while a man creating is responsible. Because the growth-fostering earth has but one will: to foster growth, whereas man must have the will to foster the growth of the good, which he knows. (It is significant that only that famous thing, "individuality," the unipersonal, can be *vicious:* there is no such thing as a vicious epic or vicious nature.)

The earth didn't eat the apple in Paradise—Adam ate it. It didn't eat, and doesn't know; he did eat—and he does know, and, knowing, is answerable. And insofar as the artist is a human being and not a monster, an animated bone-structure and not a coral bush—he must answer for the work of his hands.

Thus the work of art is the same thing as a work of nature, but one that is to be illumined by the light of reason and conscience. Then it serves the good, as a stream turning a mill-wheel serves the good. But to call every work of art good is the same as to call every stream useful. Sometimes it is useful, and sometimes harmful, and how much oftener—harmful!

It is good when you take it (take yourself) in hand.

The moral law can be grafted onto art, but can a mercenary corrupted by so many changes of master ever turn into a soldier of the regular army?

Poet and elements.

Poetry is God in the holy dreams of the earth

There is ecstasy in battle,
and on the sober chasm's edge.

146

Ecstacy, that is, intoxication, is a feeling not in itself good; it is outside goodness, and anyway—intoxication with what?

> Whatever threatens us with doom
> hides in itself, for mortal hearts,
> unspeakable pleasures—

When you speak of the sacredness of art, call to mind this confession by Pushkin.

—Well, but further on it says...

—All right. Let's dwell on that one line then, the one trump card for goodness: "...guarantee/ perhaps of immortality!" What kind of immortality? In God? In such vicinity the very sound of the word is wild to the ear. It is a guarantee of the immortality of nature itself, of the elements themselves—and of us, insofar as we *are* the elements, *are* nature. The line is clearly pagan, if not blasphemous.

And further, in black and white:

> And so, all praise to thee, O Plague!
> We're not afraid of murky tombs,
> We're not confounded by your call,
> As one we lift our frothing cups
> And drink the rose maiden's breath
> Although that breath be... breath of Plague!

Not Pushkin, the elements. Nowhere did the elements ever speak themselves out so utterly. The visitation of the elemental—no matter upon whom, today—upon Pushkin. Written in tongues of flame, in ocean waves, in desert sands—in anything at all, only not in words.

And this capital letter for Plague means plague not as a blind elemental force any longer, but as a goddess, as the proper name and visage of *evil*.

The most remarkable thing is that we all love these lines, none of us judges them. If one of us were to say such a thing in real life, or, still better, were to do it (set fire to a house, for instance, blow up a bridge), we would all come to our senses and shout: "Crime!" Yes indeed, come to our senses—out of a spell, wake up—out of a sleep, that dead sleep of conscience, within which nature's forces—our own—stay awake, the sleep into which we were cast by those few measured lines.

Genius.

The visitation of the elemental, no matter upon whom—today upon Pushkin. In the little song of the Wilson tragedy Pushkin is a genius primarily because it *came upon* him.

Genius: the highest degree of subjectedness to the visitation—one; control of that visitation—two. The highest degree of being pulled apart and the highest of—being gathered together. The highest of—passivity, and the highest—of activity.

To let oneself be annihilated right down to the last atom, from the survival (the resistance) of which will grow—a world.

For in this, this, *this* atom of resistance (ability to resist) is the whole of mankind's chance of genius. Without it there is no genius—instead there is the crushed man who (the same man!) fills to overflowing not only the Bedlams and Charentons, but also the most well-ordered households.

There is no genius without will, but still more there is none, still less is there any, without the visitation. Will is that unit to the countless millions of the elemental visitation thanks to which they alone *are* the millions (they realize their million quality) and without which they are noughts—that is, bubbles above a drowning man. The will without the visitation—in poetic creation—is just a solid post. An oaken post. Such a poet would do better to go and be a soldier.

Pushkin and Walsingham.

Walsingham was not the only one visited by the plague. To write his *The Feast during the Plague* Pushkin had to *be* Walsingham—and cease to be him. Repentant? No.

To write the "Song of the Feast," Pushkin had to fight down in himself both Walsingham and the priest and pass through into some third thing as if through a door. If he had dissolved himself into the plague, he could not have written this song. If he had warded the plague off with signs of the Cross, he could not have written this song (the link would have snapped).

From the plague (the element) Pushkin *escaped,* not into the feast (the plague's, and Walsingham's, triumphal feast over him) and not into prayer (the priest's) but into song.

Like Goethe in *Werther*, Pushkin escaped from the plague (Goethe—from love) by giving his hero the death he himself longed to die. And by putting into his mouth a song that Walsingham could not have composed.

If Walsingham had been *able* to write that song, he would have been saved, if not for life everlasting, yet at least for life. But, as we all know, Walsingham is long since upon the black cart.

Walsingham is Pushkin without the escape into song. Pushkin is Walsingham with the gift of song and the will to it.

* * *

Why do I arbitrarily identify Pushkin with Walsingham and not with the priest, whom he also created?

This is why. In the *Feast*, the priest doesn't sing. (Priests generally don't—yes, they do: prayers.) If Pushkin had been the priest as much (with the same strength) as he was Walsingham, he would not have been able to help making him sing, he'd have put into his mouth a counter-hymn—a *prayer* to the Plague—just as he put the delightful song (of love) into the mouth of Mary, who is in the Feast (while Walsingham is what Pushkin *is)* what Pushkin loves.

The lyric poet betrays himself by song, and always will, for he cannot help making his favorite (his double) speak in his own, poet's, language. A song, in a dramatic work, is always love's give-away, an unwitting sign of preference. The author tires

149

of speaking for others and gives himself away—in song.

What remains to us of the Feast (in our ears and souls)? Two songs. Mary's and Walsingham's. Of love—and of the Plague.

Pushkin's genius lies in not providing a counterweight to Walsingham's hymn, an antidote to Plague—a prayer. If he had, the work would have got—equilibrium, and we—satisfaction, and no increase of good would have come of it, since by slaking our thirst for a counter-hymn Pushkin would have extinguished it. So (with only the *hymn* to the Plague) God, the good, prayer— remain: outside, as a place to which we not only aspire but to which we are thrown back; the place to which the Plague throws us back. The prayer that Pushkin doesn't provide is here, as something inescapable. (The priest in the play speaks by rote, and not only don't we feel anything, we don't even listen to him, knowing in advance what he will say.)

Pushkin could hardly have thought of all that. One can only plan a work backwards, from the last step taken to the first, re- tracing with one's eyes open that path which one had walked blindly. *Think* the work *back.*

* * *

A poet is the reverse of a chess-player. Not only does he not see the pieces and the board, he doesn't even see his own hand— which perhaps is not there.

* * *

What does the blasphemy of Walsingham's song consist in? There is no reviling of God in it, only praise of the Plague. Yet can there be found any blasphemy mightier than that song?

The blasphemy lies not in the fact that from fear and des- pair we feast in the time of the Plague (thus children laugh from fear!) but in the fact that in song—the apogee of the feast—we have *lost* our fear, that we make of retribution a feast, turn re- tribution into a blessing, that we dissolve not in the fear of God but in the bliss of annihilation.

That is, if (as everyone believed in those days and as we too believe while we are reading Pushkin) the Plague is God's will to punish and subdue us,—if it is indeed God's scourge.

We throw ourselves under that scourge, as leaves under the sunbeam, as foliage under the rain. Not joy in the lesson but joy in the blow. Pure joy in the blow as such.

Joy? That's saying little. Bliss, which has no equal in the whole of the world's poetry. Bliss of complete surrender to the elemental force—be it Love or Plague, or whatever we call it.

For after the hymn to the Plague there was no God at all. And what else remains for the priest to do, except: having come in ("enter priest"), to go out.

The priest went away to pray, Pushkin—to sing. Pushkin goes away after the priest, he goes away last, tearing himself with effort (as if by the roots) away from his double, Walsingham, or rather at this moment Pushkin divides: into Pushkin-Walsingham and Pushkin-the-poet, himself doomed and himself saved.

And Walsingham sits at the table eternally. And Walsingham rides on the black cart eternally. And Walsingham is dug in with a spade eternally.

For the song by which Pushkin was saved.

* * *

A fearsome name—Walsingham. And there is good reason why Pushkin called him by it only three times in the whole of the play (called him by his name—like an invocation, and, like an invocation, called him thrice). The anonymous "President," which lends the work a sinister modern relevance, brings him closer.

* * *

The elements don't need Walsinghams. They defeat them in their stride. To conquer God in Walsingham is far easier, alas, than to conquer song in Pushkin.

The Plague, in *The Feast during the Plague*, coveted not Walsingham but Pushkin.

And Walsingham—*mirabile dictu!*—who is to the Plague only an occasion for getting Pushkin; Walsingham, who is for Pushkin only an occasion for his own elemental (plague-ridden) self; that very Walsingham saves Pushkin from the Plague—lets him escape into song, without which Pushkin cannot be his elemental self. Gives him the song and takes upon himself the death.

The last atom of resistance to the elemental, while glorifying it—*is* art. Nature conquering herself to her own glory.

* * *

So long as you are a poet, you shall not perish in the elemental, for everything brings you back into the element of elements: the word.

So long as you are a poet, you shall not perish in the elemental, for that is not to perish but to return to its very bosom.

Perdition, for the poet—is the abjuration of the elemental. Simpler to cut one's veins without ado.

* * *

The whole of Walsingham is an exteriorization (a carrying outside his limits) of the elemental Pushkin. You cannot live with a Walsingham inside you: it means either a crime or a poem. Even if Walsingham *existed*—Pushkin would still have *created* him.

* * *

Thank the Lord the poet has the hero, the third person—*him*—as a way out. Otherwise—what a shameful (and continuous) confession.

Thus at least appearances are preserved.

* * *

The "Apollonian principle," the "golden mean"—surely you see this is nothing more than bits of Latin stuck in the schoolboy's head.

Pushkin, who created Walsingham, Pugachov, Mazeppa, Peter, who created them from inside himself, who didn't create them but disgorged them...

The Pushkin of the sea, "of the free element."

—There was also another Pushkin.

—Yes: the Pushkin of the Walsingham sunk in thought.

(Exit Priest. The President remains, sunk in deep thought.)

* * *

November 1830. Boldino. A hundred years ago. A hundred years later.

* * *

Art's Lessons.

What does art teach? Goodness? No. Common sense? No. It cannot even teach itself, for it is given.

There is no thing which is not taught by art; there is no thing directly the reverse of that which is not taught by art; and no thing is the only thing which is taught by art.

All the lessons which we derive from art, *we* put into it.

A series of answers to which there are no questions.

All art is the sole givenness of the answer.

Thus, in *The Feast during the Plague* it answered before I asked, it showered me with answers.

All *our* art is in being able (managing in time) to oppose to each answer, before it evaporates, *our* question. This being out-galloped by answers is what inspiration is. And how often—a blank page.

* * *

One reads *Werther* and shoots himself, another reads *Werther* and, because Werther shoots himself, decides to live. One has acted like Werther, the other like Goethe. A lesson in self-destruction? A lesson in self-defense? Both. Goethe, by some law of that hour of his life, *needed* to shoot Werther,—and the suicidal demon of the generation needed to be incarnated precisely through Goethe's hand. A twice fated necessity and as such—devoid of responsibility. And *very* fraught with consequences.

Is Goethe guilty of all the consequent deaths?

He himself in his profound and splendid old age, replied: *no.* Otherwise we wouldn't dare say a word, for who can calculate the effect of any one word? (I'm putting it my own way, but this is the gist of it.)

I too shall reply for Goethe: no.

He had no evil will, he had no will at all, except the creative one. Writing his *Werther,* he not only forgot all the others (that is, their possible calamities) but forgot himself too (his own calamity!).

All-forgetfulness—that is, forgetfulness of everything which is not the work—that is, the very basis of creation.

Would Goethe have written *Werther* a second time after everything that had happened, if (improbably) he had again had just as desperate a need to—and would he then have been indictable? Would Goethe have written—knowingly?

He would have written it a thousand times if he had needed to, but he would not have written a single line of the first one if the pressure had been the tiniest bit lighter. (Werther, like Walsingham, is a pressure from within.)

—And would he then have been indictable?

As a man—yes. As an artist—no.

Moreover: as an artist, Goethe would have been both indictable and condemned if he had immolated Werther within himself in order to preserve human lives (to fulfill the commandment: thou shalt not kill). Here the law of art is the direct reverse of the moral law. An artist is guilty only in two cases: that of the refusal (mentioned already) to create a work of art (for whomever's sake) and that of the creation of an inartistic work. Here his lesser responsibility ends and here begins his boundless responsibility as a human being.

In some cases artistic creation is a sort of atrophy of conscience—more than that: a necessary atrophy of conscience, the moral flaw without which art can never exist. In order to be good (and not lead into temptation the little ones of this world) art would have to renounce a good half of itself. The only way for art to be wittingly good is not to be. It will come to an end when the life of the planet ends.

* * *

Tolstoi's Crusade.

"An exception in favor of genius." Our whole relation to art is an exception in favor of genius. Art itself is that genius in favor of which we are excepted (we are exempted) from the moral law.

What is our whole attitude to art if not this: conquerors are not to be judged; and what else is art but a foreknown conqueror (seducer)—of our conscience above all.

The reason why, despite all our love for art, we so hotly respond to the clumsy, extra-aesthetic (for he went and he led against his own grain) challenge thrown by Tolstoi to art, is that this challenge comes from the lips of an artist, from seduced and seducing lips.

In Tolstoi's call for the destruction of art, what is important is the mouth that does the calling: if it did not sound from such a head-turning artistic height—if it were any one of *us* calling us—we would not even turn our heads.

In Tolstoi's crusade against art what is important is Tolstoi: the artist. We *forgive* the artist the shoemaker. *War and Peace* cannot be eradicated from our attitude to him. Ineradicable. Unalterable. We *consecrate* the shoemaker, through the artist.

In Tolstoi's crusade against art we are once again seduced— by art.

* * *

All this is not a reproach to Tolstoi, but a reproach to us, the slaves of art. Tolstoi would have given his soul to make people listen not to Tolstoi but to *the truth.*

* * *

Objection.

Whose preaching of poverty is more convincing, that is, more deadly to wealth—that of the man who is poor from birth, or that of the rich man who has renounced his riches?

The latter, of course.

The same applies to Tolstoi. Whose condemnation of pure art is more convincing (more deadly to art)—that of the Tolstoian who has been nothing in art, or that of Tolstoi himself—who has been everything?

Thus, having begun by placing our eternal credit with Tolstoi the artist, we end with the recognition of the complete discrediting—by Tolstoi the artist—of art itself.

* * *

When I think of the moral essence of that species of human being, the poet, I always recall the definition of the Tolstoi father in *Childhood* and *Boyhood.* "He belonged to that dangerous breed of people who are able to narrate one and the same action as the greatest baseness and as the most innocent joke."

The Sleeper.

Let us return to Goethe. Goethe in his *Werther* is just as innocent of the evil (the destruction of lives) as (example of the second reader who as a result of *Werther* decides to live) innocent of the good. Both—death *and* desire to live— are to be seen as consequence, not purpose.

When Goethe had a *purpose* he realized it in his life, that is, he built a theater, proposed to Karl-August a series of reforms, studied the customs and soul of the ghetto, studied mineralogy,— in short, whenever Goethe had some purpose or other he realized it directly, without this great roundabout way of art.

The sole purpose of a work of art at the time of its being

made is that it should be completed: and not just that the work as a whole should be completed, but each separate particle of it, each molecule. It itself, as a whole, steps back before the realization of this molecule, or better, each molecule *is* this whole, whose purpose is there in its entire length and breadth, ubiquitous, omnipresent, and it itself, the whole, is an end-in-itself.

At its completion it may turn out that the artist has made something bigger than he had planned *(could,* more than he thought!), something different from what he planned. Or others will say so—as they said to Blok. And Blok was always astonished and always agreed with everyone, agreed practically with the first comer, so new to him was all this (that is, the presence of any purpose at all).

Blok's "The Twelve" arose under a spell. The demon of that particular hour of the Revolution (which *is* Blok's "music of the revolution") inhabited Blok and compelled him.

And the naive moralizer Zinaida Gippius then spent a long time wondering whether or not to shake hands with Blok, while he patiently waited.

Blok wrote "The Twelve" in one night and got up in complete exhaustion like one who has been driven upon.

Blok did not know "The Twelve," never read it from a platform ("I don't know 'The Twelve.' I don't remember 'The Twelve'." Really, he *did not know.)*

And his terror is understandable, when in the year 1920 on the Vozdvizhenka he seized the hand of his companion:

"Look!"

And only five paces later:

"Katka!"

In the Middle Ages (yet what *extreme* ones!), whole villages, possessed by a demon, suddenly began to speak in Latin.

A poet? A sleeper.

Art in the Light of Conscience.

One of these sleepers woke up. A sharp-nosed, waxen-faced

man, who burned in the hearth of the Sheremetiev house a manuscript. The second part of *Dead Souls.*

Lead not into temptation. More than medieval—the casting of his creation to the flames by *his own hand.* That self-judgment of which I say that it is the only judgment.

(The shame and failure of the Inquisition lies in the fact that it did the burning itself instead of leading people to the point of burning things; burned manuscripts, when it should have burned out the soul.)

—But Gogol was already mad by that time.

A madman is one who burns down a temple (which he did not build) to achieve fame. Gogol, burning the work of his own hands, burned his fame too.

And I recall the words of a shoemaker (in Moscow, 1920)—a case where the shoemaker is really higher than the artist.

—It is not you and I, Marina Ivanovna, who are out of our minds, but they who are short of mind.

* * *

Gogol's half hour at the fireplace did more for good and against art than all the many-year-long preaching of Tolstoi.

Because here is a deed, a visible deed of the hands, that movement of the hand which we all thirst for, and which cannot be out-weighed by *any* "movement of the spirit."

* * *

Perhaps we would not have been tempted after all by the second part of *Dead Souls.* Undoubtedly we should have been glad to have it. But this gladness of ours is nothing before our gladness in Gogol, who out of love for our living souls burned his *Dead* ones. On the fire of his own conscience.

The first were written with ink.

The second—in us—with fire.

Art without Novitiate.

Yet there are works, in the very depths of art, and simultaneously upon its heights, of which one wants to say: "This isn't art any more. This is more than art." Everyone has known works of this sort.

A sign of them is their active power despite the inadequacy of means, an inadequacy which nothing in the world would make us exchange for any adequacies and abundances and which we only think of when we try to establish: how was it done. (An essentially futile approach, for in every born work the ends are hidden.)

Not yet art, and already more than art.

Such works often come from the pens of women, children, self-taught people,—the little ones of this world. And often they come from no pen at all, being unwritten but preserved (or lost) orally. Often they are the only works of a lifetime. Often—the very first. Often—the very last.

Art without novitiate.

Here is a poem by a four-year-old boy who did not live long.

A white bird is living there,
A pale boy is walking there.
Surely! Surely! Surely!
It really is—over there.

("Vedno" [surely]—a child's and folk form of "vedomo" [known] which here sounds both like "verno" [right] and "za-vedomo" [wittingly]: wittingly right. While "tam—ot" [over there] is a nanny's word for far away.)

Here is the last line of a little poem by a seven-year-old girl who had never walked and who prays to be able to stand up. I only heard the poem once, twenty years ago, and I remember only the last line: "So that I may *stand up* and pray!"

And here is a poem by a nun at the Novo-Devichy Convent —she had many poems and burned them all before she died; one of them remained and is alive today, in my memory only. I pass it on, as a good deed.

> Whatever life may keep in store,
> Dear children, there will be much sorrow,
> The crafty nets of temptation,
> The darkness of burning repentance,
> The yearning of hopeless desires,
> And cheerless unending toil,
> And a dozen moments of happiness,
> Paid for with years of suffering—
> Yet do not weaken in spirit,
> In time of tribulations—
> Mankind is solely alive
> Through the round robin of good!
> Wherever your heart bids you live,
> In world's bustle or country quiet,
> Pour out fearlessly and freely
> The treasures of your soul!
> Don't seek or expect a return,
> Nor let cruel jibes disturb you,
> Mankind is solely rich
> In the round robin of good!

If we take the rhymes, they are undeniably commonplace, undeniably weak. Or the meter—it too has nothing compelling to the ear. With what means was this undeniably great thing made?

—With no means. With the bare soul.

This unknown nun of a permanently lost nunnery has given the fullest definition of good that has ever existed: *"goodness as a round robin,"* and has flung the most unmalicious challenge to evil ever heard upon earth:

> Wherever your heart bids you live,

In world's bustle or country quiet,

(A nun speaking, confined to her nunnery!)

> Pour out fearlessly and freely
> The treasures of your soul!

To say these lines have "genius" would be blasphemy, and to judge them as a literary work—a mere trifle, so far is all that beyond the threshold of this *great* (as earthly love is) *trifle of art.*

I have quoted what I remember. I am convinced there is more. (I deliberately pass over the poems of my own six-year-old daughter, some of which were published at the end of my book *Psyche,* as I mean to speak of them separately sometime.) But even suppose there *were* no more! Here, in *my* memory alone, are three poems which are more than poems.

Or perhaps only this sort of verse is true verse?

* * *

A sign of such works is their unevenness. Take the nun's poem.

Whatever life may keep in store, —Dear Children, there will be much sorrow, —The crafty nets of temptation, —The darkness of burning repentance (so far it is all cliché). —The yearning of hopeless desires, —And cheerless unending toil, (still the same) —And a dozen moments of happiness—Paid for with years of suffering (this last bit is almost a parlor song) — Yet do not weaken in spirit, —In time of tribulations—

And—here it comes!—

> Mankind is solely alive
> In the round robin of good!

Then on, up a continuous line of ascent that never falters, in one great profound sigh to the very end.

This at first glance (already mentioned) commonplace

beginning was needed by her as a run-up, so she could talk her way up to the round robin of good. Inexperience of the non-professional. A real poet, the kind our capitals teem with, if he had, beyond expectation, written his way up to the round robin (but he never would!), would not have kept that beginning but would have tried to fit everything to one common level of loftiness.

Whereas the nun did not even notice the insufficiency of the beginning, for neither did she notice the round robin—perhaps vaguely glad of it as of something very *like*—but no more. For my nun is not a professional poet who would sell his soul to the devil for an effective turn of phrase (though the devil would not take it—there's nothing there to take)—but: —a pure vessel of God, that is, just the same as that four-year-old with his "over there," and all of them: the nun, the little girl without legs, the little boy,—and all the nameless little girls, boys, nuns of the world— say one thing, speak of one thing, or rather, that one thing speaks out through them.

These are my favorite poems of all those I have ever read, or ever written, the ones I love best of all poems on earth. When I read (or write) my own after reading them I feel nothing but shame.

I'd also place among such poems the poem "Thought" (stoned to death many a time) by an unknown author, signed, in all the collections where it was printed, with the single letter D.

Thus with this capital D (for "dobro" [goodness]) these poems have gone onward.

Attempt at a Hierarchy.

A significant poet. A great poet. A lofty poet.

A significant poet is what anyone—any significant poet—can be. To be a significant poet it is enough to have a poetic gift of significance. To be a great poet, even the most significant gift is too small—he needs an equivalent gift of personality—of mind, soul and will—and the aspiration of the whole personality towards a definite aim; that is, its organization. But a lofty poet is something that even a quite insignficant poet, bearer of the most modest gift, can be—like, say, Alfred de Vigny—by the power of his inner worth alone winning our recognition as a poet. In that case the gift was just big enough. A little less and he'd only have been a hero (which is immeasurably more).

The great poet includes the lofty poet—and counterbalances him. The lofty poet does *not* include the great one, or else we would call him great. Loftiness—as the sole sign of existence. Thus, there is no poet more significant than Goethe, but there are poets who are loftier,—his younger contemporary Hölderlin for instance, an incomparably poorer poet, yet a native dweller upon those heights where Goethe is but a guest. For a *lofty* poet is less than a great one, even if they are of equal height. Just as the oak is great, the cypress lofty.

The earthly foundation of genius is too large and stable to let it disappear into loftiness. Shakespeare, Goethe, Pushkin. Had Shakespeare, Goethe, Pushkin been loftier they would have left many a thing unheard, unanswered, would just not have condescended to many things.

Genius: the resultant force of two counteractions, that is, ultimately, equilibrium, that is, harmony; while the giraffe is a freak, a creature of one dimension only: his own neck; the giraffe *is* neck. (Every freak is but a part of himself.)

That "the poet dwells among the clouds" is true, but true only of one breed of poet: the one who is only lofty, the purely spiritual one. And he doesn't dwell, he inhabits. The humpback pays for his hump, the angel too pays for his wings upon earth. Fleshlessness, so near to fruitlessness, rarefied air, thought instead of passion, utterances instead of words—these are the earthly signs of heavenly guests.

A sole exception—Rilke, a poet not only equally lofty and great (this can be said of Goethe too) but having that same exclusive loftiness which in his case excludes nothing. As if God—who, when giving other poets of the spirit their one gift, took everything else away from them—*left* to this one that everything else. Into the bargain.

* * *

Loftiness as equality does not exist. Only as primacy.

* * *

For the merely significant poet art is always an aim in itself, that is, a mere function without which he cannot live and for which he is not responsible. For the great poet and the lofty poet it is always a means. He himself is a means in someone's hands, as indeed the merely significant poet is, too—in other hands. The whole difference, apart from the basic difference of which hands, is in the degree of consciousness the poet has of his being held. The spiritually greater the poet, that is, the loftier the hands holding him, the more powerfully conscious he is of this being-held (his being in service).

If Goethe had not known a higher force above himself and his work he would never have written the last lines of the last *Faust*. Only to the innocent is it given—or to one who knows *everything*.

Essentially, the whole of a poet's labor is but an act of fulfilling, the physical fulfilling of a spiritual task (not assigned by himself). Just as the whole of the poet's will is but the laboring will to bring into existence. (There is no such thing as a personal creative will.) It is the will to embody physically what already e-xists spiritually (the eternal) and to embody spiritually (to inspirit) what does not yet exist spiritually and desires to, regardless of the qualities of the desirer. To embody the spirit that desires a body (ideas), and to inspirit the bodies that desire a soul (the elements). The word is body to ideas, soul to the elements.

Every poet is, in some way or other, the servant of ideas or of the elements. Sometimes (as already mentioned)—of ideas alone. Sometimes—of both ideas and the elements. Sometimes—of the elements alone. But even in this last case he is still *the first low sky of something:* the sky of those very elements and passions. Through the element of the word, which alone among all the elements, is from its very beginning made sense of, that is, made spirit of. *The low close sky of the earth.*

* * *

In this ethical approach (the demand for an idea-content, that is, loftiness, in a writer) there may lie the whole solution to something which is at first glance incomprehensible, the Nineties' preferring Nadson to Pushkin, who is, if not obviously idea-less, certainly less obviously idea-ful than Nadson, and the previous generation's preferring Nekrasov the citizen to just Nekrasov. All that fierce utilitarianism, all the Bazarovism—is only the affirmation of and demand for loftiness as the first foundation of life—*only the Russian aspect of loftiness.* Our utilitarianism is whatever is useful to the spirit. Our "usefulness" is only conscience. Russia, to her honor, or rather to the honor of her conscience and not to the honor of her artistry (two things that do not need each other), has always approached writers—or rather, always *went* to writers—as the peasant went to the Tsar—for the truth, and it was good when the Tsar turned out to be Lev Tolstoi, and not Artsybashev. For Russia learned to live from Artsybashev's Sanin as well!

Prayer.

What can we say about God? Nothing. What can we say to God? Everything. Poems to God are prayer. And if at the moment there are no prayers (except for Rilke and those of the little ones, I do not know any prayers), then it is not because we have nothing to say to God and not because we have no one to say this *something* to—there is something and there is someone— but because we haven't the conscience to praise and pray to God in that same language in which we praised and prayed to absolutely everything for centuries. To have the daring, in our age, for direct speech to God (for prayer) we must either not know what poems are, or—forget.

Loss of trust.

The cruel thing Blok said about the early Akhmatova: Akhmatova writes poems as if a man were looking at her, but you should write them as if God were looking at you (remoulding the first, denunciatory half of the sentence to fit each one of us)—in the end, holily. As if before God, that is, *standing in the divine presence.*

But what in us shall then withstand, and who among us?

Point of View.

In relation to the spiritual world art is a sort of physical world of the spiritual. In relation to the physical world, art is a sort of spiritual world of the physical.

Starting from the earth it is the first millimeter of air above it (that is, of sky, for the sky begins immediately above the earth, or else there is no sky at all. Verify this by distances, which clarify phenomena).

Starting from the top of the sky, it is this same first millimeter above the earth, but the last when seen from above, that is, it is now almost earth, and from the very top it is entirely earth.

It depends where you look from.

* * *

(Likewise the soul, which the common man regards as the acme of spirituality, is for the spiritual man—almost flesh. The analogy with art is not accidental, for poetry—which I have constantly in mind when I say art—the whole happening of verse —from the visitation to the poet to the reader's reception—takes place wholly in the soul, in that very first and lowest sky of the spirit. Which is in no way contradictory to art—to nature. There is no soul-less nature—there is only spirit-less nature.

Poet, Poet! The most soul-ful—and how often (perhaps just *because* so filled with soul) the most spirit-less object!)

* * *

Fier quand je me compare—no! because whatever is below a poet does not count: he still has enough pride not to level himself down. For I look up from below and my point of support is not in my own lowness but in that height. *Humble quand je me compare, inconnu quand je me considère,* for in order to contemplate something one must rise above the thing contemplated; one must place between oneself and the thing all the vertical steepness—refusal—of height. For indeed I do look down from above! The highest in me—looks at the lowest in me. And what do I keep of this confrontation—except amazement or recognition.

> She took the faded pages
> And gazed upon them strangely
> As souls look from on high
> At bodies they've cast off.

So one day shall I, indeed I sometimes do already, look at my poems.

The Poet's Heaven.

—A priest serves God in his way, you—in yours.

—Blasphemy. When I write my poem *A Lad*—love of a vampire for a girl and hers for him—I do not serve any god: I know what god I serve. When I describe the Tatars in the wide-open spaces I again do not serve any god, except the wind (or a wizard: my forebear). All my Russian works are elemental—that is, sinful. One must be aware what forces are at play. When shall we finally stop taking strength for truth and magic for holiness!

Art is a test, perhaps the last, subtlest, most insuperable of the earth's temptations, that last small cloud in the last sky, at which—dying, no longer looking at anything, struggling to get its hue into words—having already forgotten all words, that *brother of his brother,* Jules Goncourt, gazed.

The third kingdom with its laws from which we so seldom escape into the higher (and so often into the lower!). The third kingdom, the first sky above the earth, is a second earth. Between the heaven of the spirit and the hell of our kind, art is a purgatory which no one wishes to leave for paradise.

When I see a priest, a monk, or even a nurse—I lower my eyes—invariably—irresistibly! I know why I lower my eyes. My shame at the sight of a priest, a monk, even a nurse—that shame is visionary.

—You are doing God's work.

—If the things I write help to renounce, enlighten, purify— yes; but if they seduce—no, and I'd rather have a stone tied round my neck.

And how often in one and the same work, on one and the same page, in one and the same line, are both renunciation and seduction. Like the dubious swill in the witches' cauldron—what was *not* flung into this brew?

* * *

How many it destroyed, how few it saved!

* * *

And the immediate riposte of the accused:

> Dark power!
> Craft of Mra!
> How many—destroyed!
> How few—saved!

I am afraid that even when I am dying... The word "Mra," by the way, I take here as a feminine noun, a feminine ending, the very sound of death. "Mor" (masculine), "Mra" (feminine). Death could have been, and perhaps at some time somewhere *was*, called "Mra." Word-creation, like any creation, is only a journeying in the track of the hearing ear of nation and nature. A journey by ear. *Et tout le reste n'est que littérature.*

* * *

Polytheism of the poet. I should say that our Christian God makes *at best one* of the host of his gods. Never an atheist. Always à polytheist, with the one difference that the higher knows the older (knows what there was, even in the time of the pagans).

The majority, however, do not know even this and blindly put Christ and Dionysus in any old order, not realizing that the very juxtaposition of these names is blasphemy and sacrilege.

Art would be holy, if *we* lived in that time, or if those gods lived in our time. The poet's heaven is exactly on a level with the pedestal of Zeus: the summit of Olympus.

The Kernel of the Kernel.

> ...and you send reply.
> But to you there is no response... Such
> Are you, too, poet!

Not-poet, above-poet, more than poet, not only a poet—but where is the *poet* then in all this? *Der Kern des Kernes,* the kernel of the kernel.

A poet is the answer.

From the lowest level of the simple reflex to the highest level of Goethe's great answer—the poet is a definite and unchanging spiritual-artistic reflex: to what—this is already a question, perhaps simply of brain capacity. Pushkin said: to everything. The answer of a genius.

This spiritual-artistic reflex is the kernel of the kernel, uniting the anonymous author of a chastushka with the author of *Faust, Part Two.* Without it there is no poet, or rather, the poet is *it.* Miracle of the poet, not explainable by any convolutions of the brain.

A reflex before any thought, even before any feeling, the deepest and fastest—as if by electric current—spearing of the whole being by a given phenomenon and the simultaneous, almost preceding it, answer to it.

Answer not to the blow, but to the stirring of the air—of

a thing that has not yet moved. Answer to the pre-blow. And not an answer, but a pre-answer. Always to a phenomenon, never to a question. The very phenomenon is the question. The thing self-strikes the poet—with itself, self-questions him—with itself. Command for an answer given by the phenomenon itself—that has not yet been revealed and is revealed only through the answer. Command? Yes, if S.O.S. is a command (the most un-repulsable of all).

Before it existed. (It always did exist, only it had not yet got as far as time—in the same way: the opposite shore has not yet reached the ferry.) The reason why the poet's hand is so often arrested in mid-air is that the support for it—in time—does not yet exist. *Nicht vorhanden.*

The poet's hand—even if arrested in mid-air!—creates the phenomenon (completes the creation of it). This hand arrested in the air *is* the poet's uncompleted, despairing, yet still creative, yet still: *"be."* (Who called me? —Silence. —I must create the one who called me, that is—name him. Such is the poet's "respond-ing.")

One more thing. "Spiritual-artistic reflex." Artistic-vulneral, for our soul is the capacity for pain—and that's all. (For pain—not in the head, not in the tooth, not in the throat, not—not—not etc., pain, and that's all.)

This is the kernel of the kernel of the poet—leaving aside the *indispensable* artistry—the *strength of anguish.*

The Truth of Poets.

Such then is the truth of poets, the most invincible, the most elusive, the most bereft of proof and the most convincing, a truth that lives in us only the length of a sort of first *glimmer* of perception (what was that?) and remains in us only as the trace of light or a loss (was anything there at all?). A truth with-out responsibility or consequence, which—for God's sake—one should not even attempt to pursue because even for the poet it is irretrievable. (A poet's truth is a path where all traces are straightaway overgrown.) Untraceable even for the poet himself, were he to follow in his own wake. He didn't know what he was going to say, and often didn't know what he was saying. Didn't know till he had said it, and forgot it the moment it was said. Not one amongst innumerable truths but one of the innumerable countenances of the truth, which destroy each other only when they are set side by side. Once-only aspects of the truth. Just a needle-prick in the heart of Eternity. The means: juxtaposition of two most ordinary words, which place themselves side by side just so. (Sometimes—divided by a single hyphen!)

There is a lock which opens only by means of a certain combination of figures; when you know the combination you can open it, when you don't—then only by a miracle or chance. A miracle-chance, which incidentally, happened to my six-year-old son who at one go twisted and unfastened a fine chain that had been locked around his neck, thereby throwing the owner of the chain into horror. Does the poet know, or doesn't he, the combination of figures? (In the case of the poet—for all the world is under a lock and everything waits to be unlocked—it is different every time, each thing has its own lock, behind the lock is a given truth, each time different, a once-only truth—like the lock itself.) Does the poet know all the combinations?

* * *

My mother had a certain peculiarity of setting the clock during the night, whenever it stopped. In answer to its silence instead of ticking, which is what probably woke her up, she would set it in the dark without looking. In the morning the clock showed *the time*—that absolute time, I suppose, which was never found by that unhappy crowned contemplator of so many contradictory clock-faces and listener to so many discrepant chimes.

The clock showed *the time*.

* * *

Chance? a chance that is repeated every time is—in the life

171

of a man: fate, —in the world of phenomena: law. This was the law of her hand. The law of her hand's *knowledge*.

Not—"my mother had a peculiarity," but—her hand had the peculiarity—of truth.

Not playing like my son, not self-assured like the owner of the lock, and not visionary like the imaginary mathematician, but—both blind and visionary—obeying only his hand (which—itself—obeys what?): that is how the poet opens the lock.

There is only one gesture he lacks: the self-assured, sure of self and of lock alike, gesture of the owner of the lock. A poet does not possess a single lock as his own. That is why he unlocks them all. And that is why, unlocking each at the first try, he will not open any of them a second time. Because he is not the owner of the secret but only its passer-by.

The Condition of Creation.

The condition of creation is a condition of being overcome by a spell. Until you begin, it is a state of being obsessed; until you finish, a state of being possessed. Something, someone, lodges in you, your hand is the fulfiller not of you but of *him*. Who is he? That which through you wants to be.

Things always chose me by the mark of my strength and often I wrote them almost against my will. All of my Russian works are like this. Certain things of Russia wanted to be spoken, they chose me. And they persuaded, seduced me—by what? by my own strength; "only you!" Yes, only I. And having given in—sometimes seeingly, sometimes blindly—I obeyed, sought out with my ear some prescribed aural lesson. And it is not I that from a hundred words (not rhymes! in the middle of a line) would choose the hundred and first, but it (the thing), resisting all the hundred epithets: that isn't what *I'm* called.

The condition of creation is a condition of dreaming, when suddenly, obeying an unknown necessity, you set fire to a house or push your friend down from a mountain-top. Is it *your* act? Clearly it is yours (it is you, after all, that is sleeping, dreaming!).

Yours—in complete freedom, the act of yourself without conscience, of yourself as nature.

A series of doors, behind one of which someone—something (more often something terrible) is waiting. The doors are identical. Not this one—not this one—not this one—*that* one. Who told me? No one. I recognize the one I need by all the unrecognized ones (the right one by all the wrong ones). So it is with words too. Not this one—not this one—not this one—*that* one. By the obviousness of the wrong I recognize the right. Native to every sleeper and writer is the *blow of recognition*. O, the sleeper cannot be deceived! He knows friend and he knows enemy, knows the door and knows the chasm behind the door—and to all this: both friend and enemy and door and pit—he is doomed. The sleeper cannot be deceived even by the sleeper himself. Vainly I say to myself: I won't go in (through the door), I won't look (through the window)—I know that I shall go in, and even while I am saying: I won't look, I am looking.

O, the sleeper is not to be saved!

There is, though, even in sleep a loop-hole. When it is too terrible, I shall wake up. In sleep—I shall wake up, in poetry—I shall resist.

Someone said to me about the poems of Pasternak: splendid poems when you explain them all like that, but one ought to supply a key with them.

No, not supply a key with the poems (dreams), the poems themselves are a key to the understanding of everything. But from understanding to accepting there is not one step, there is no step at all; to understand *is* to accept, there is no other kind of understanding, every other kind of understanding is non-understanding. Not for nothing is the French "comprendre" at the same time both to understand and to encompass, that is—to have accepted, to include.

There is no poet who would reject *any* elemental force—or, consequently, any rebellion. Pushkin feared Nicholas, deified Peter, but loved—Pugachov. It wasn't by chance that all the pupils of one remarkable and wrongly forgotten poetess, who was also a teacher of history, answered the question put by the district superintendent: "Well, children, and who is your favorite tsar?" (the whole class in one voice together)—"Grishka Otrepev!"

Find me a poet without a Pugachov! without an Imposter! without a Corsican!—*inside* him. A poet might simply lack the strength (the means) for a Pugachov. *Mais l'intention y est—toujours.*

What doesn't accept (rejects, and even—ejects) is the human being: —will, reason, conscience.

In this realm the poet can have only one prayer: not to understand the unacceptable: let me not understand, that I be not seduced; the sole prayer of the poet is not to hear the voices: let me not hear, that I may not answer. For to hear is, for the poet, to answer, and to answer is to affirm, even if by the passionateness of his denial. The only prayer of the poet is a prayer for deafness. Or else he has the utterly difficult choice of what to hear, according to its quality, that is, the forcible stopping of his ears—to a series of calls, invariably the strongest ones. Innate selection, that is the hearing only of what is important, is a blessing given almost to no one.

(On the ship of Odysseus there was neither hero nor poet. A hero is one who will stand firm even when not tied down, will stand firm even without wax in his ears, a poet is one who will fling himself forward even when tied down, who even with wax in his ears will hear—that is, once again, will fling himself forward.

The only thing innately non-understood by the poet is the half-measure of the rope and the wax.)

Mayakovsky failed to overcome the poet in himself and the result was a monument raised by the most revolutionary of poets to the Volunteer leader. (The poem "Crimea," twelve immortal lines). I cannot help remarking the devilish cunning of whatever force it is that picks itself a herald from among its very enemies. But of course that last Crimea had to be presented—by Mayakovsky!

When at the age of thirteen I asked an old revolutionary: Is

174

it possible to be a poet and also be in the Party? —he replied, without a moment's thought: —No.

Thus I too shall answer: —No.

* * *

What element then, was it, what demon lodged at that hour in Mayakovsky and made him describe Vrangel? For the Volunteer movement, everyone now recognizes, was not elemental. (Unless perhaps—the steppe they went over, the songs they sang...)

Not the White movement, but the Black Sea was; into which, three times kissing the Russian earth, stepped the Commander-in-chief.

The Black Sea of that hour.

* * *

I don't want to serve as a springboard for the ideas of others, a loudspeaker for other people's passions.

Other people's? But is there anything *alien* to the poet? Pushkin in *The Covetous Knight* made even miserliness his own, in Salieri even untalentedness. And it was not by being alien, but in fact by being related, that Pugachov knocked at my imagination.

I shall say then: I don't want anything not wholly mine, not wittingly mine, not the most mine of all.

And what if the most mine of all (revelation of dream)—*is* Pugachov?

I want nothing that I will not answer for at seven o'clock in the morning and for which (without which) I will not die at any hour of the day or night. I won't die for Pugachov—that means he is *not something of mine.*

* * *

The reverse extreme of nature is Christ.
The other end of the road is Christ.
Everything in between is—halfway along.

And it is not for the poet, wayless from birth, to give up his waylessness—the native cross of his crossroads! —for the halfway roads of social issues or whatever else.

To lay down one's soul for one's brethren.

This is the only thing that *can* overpower the elemental in a poet.

Intoxiqués.

> —*When I find myself among literary people, artists and so on... I always have the feeling that I am among...intoxiqués.*
> —*Yes, but when you are with a great artist, a great poet, you won't say that; on the contrary, all the rest will seem to you poisoned.*
>
> *(Conversation after a literary meeting.)*

When I speak of the possessed condition of people of art, I don't at all mean that they are possessed *by art*.

Art is that through which the elemental force holds—and overpowers: it is a means for the holding (of us—by the elements), and not an autarchy; the condition of being possessed, not the content of the possessed condition.

It is not by the work of his own two hands that the sculptor is possessed and not by the work of his one hand that the poet is.

To be possessed by the work of one's own hands is to be held in someone's hands.

This applies to great artists.

But the being possessed by art does happen, for there does exist—and in immensely greater numbers than the poet—the pseudo-poet, the esthete, the one who has taken a gulp of art, not of the elemental, a creature lost both to God and to man—and lost in vain.

The demon (the elemental) pays its victim. You give me blood, life, conscience, honor, and I will give you such consciousness of strength (for strength is mine!), such freedom—within my grip—that every other strength will be laughable to you, every other power will be small, every other freedom—constricting.

—and every other prison—spacious.

Art does not pay its victims. It does not even know them.

176

The worker is paid by the master, not by the lathe. The lathe can only leave you without an arm. How many of them I have seen, poets without an arm. With an arm lost for any other work.

* * *

The shyness of the artist before the work. He forgets that it is *not himself* writing. What Vyacheslav Ivanov said to me (in 1920, in Moscow, persuading me to write a novel): "Just begin! By the third page you'll be convinced there is no freedom"— that is: I shall find myself in the power of things, that is, in the power of the demon, that is, only a humble servant.

To forget oneself is above all to forget one's weakness.

Who has ever *been able* to do anything at all with his own two hands?

To let the ear hear, the hand race (and when it doesn't race —to *let it stop*).

Not for nothing does each of us say at the end: "How wonderfully it has come out!" and never: "How wonderfully I have done it!" Not "came out wonderfully" but—came out by a wonder, always came out by a wonder, a miracle, it's always a blessing, even if sent not by God.

—And the amount of will in all this? O, enormous. Even not to despair when you wait by the sea for good weather.

Out of a hundred lines ten are—given, ninety—task-written: unyielding, then yielding, surrendering themselves like a fortress —which I fought for, got by dint of listening. And listening is what my will *is,* not to weary of listening until I hear, and not to put down anything I didn't hear. Not to be afraid of the rough-work page (crisscrossed in vain searches), nor of the blank page, but of one's *own,* self-willed, page.

Creative will is patience.

Parenthesis About A Species of Hearing.

This hearing is not allegorical, though not physical either.

So far is it from physical that you don't hear any words at all, or if you do you don't understand them, like someone half-asleep. The physical hearing either sleeps or fails to carry, replaced by other hearing.

I hear not words but a sort of soundless tune inside my head, a kind of aural line—from a hint to a command, but this is too long to tell now—it is a whole separate world, and to tell of it—a whole separate duty. Only, I am convinced that here too, as in everything, there is a law.

In the meantime: authentic hearing without any ears, which is one more proof of that:

—It really *is*—over there!

* * *

The pseudo-poet considers art to be God, and himself makes this God (moreover expecting Him to send rain!).

The pseudo-poet always does things himself.

The sign of pseudo-poetry: absence of *given* lines.

There are great experts among them.

But it happens both to poets and to geniuses.

In the "Hymn to the Plague" there are lines that are solely from the author—these:

> And happy the one who finds and knows
> those pleasures mid this turbulence.

Pushkin, released by the demon for a second, did not have the patience. This is precisely what happens when we discover in our own or other people's poetry a stop-gap line, that poetic "water" which is nothing other than the *shallows of inspiration*.

Let us take the whole passage:

> There is an ecstasy in battle,
> and on the somber chasm's edge,
> and in the ragings of the ocean,
> terrible waves and thundering dark,

and in the Arabian hurricane,
and in the breathing of the Plague.
Whatever threatens us with doom
hides in itself, for mortal hearts,
unspeakable pleasures—guarantee
perhaps of immortality!
And happy the one who finds and knows
those pleasures mid this turbulence.

Let us take it word by word:

"and happy the one"—too small! small and flabby after those absolutes of pleasure and ecstasy, an obvious repetition, a weakening, a slackening;—"mid this turbulence"—what kind of? and again what a small word (and thing)! After all the hurricanes and abysses! An allegory of worldly turbulence after the utter reality of ocean waves. "...the one who finds and knows"—finds inexpressible delights—is this German? At any rate it's not Pushkinian and not Russian. Next: "and knows" (a repetition, for in finding them one already knows them). And how, in a situation like *that,* could one *help* obtaining them? A gallicism: *heureux celui qui a pu les connâitre,* and altogether—a piece of philosophizing, *preposterous* in such a whirlwind.

That is what happens when the hand overtakes the hearing.

* * *

Back to pseudo-poets.

Pseudo-poet. Poet. Victim of literature. Victim of the demon. Both—lost to God (to the cause, to the good), but if one has to be lost then let it be honorably, and if one must accept subjugation, then let it be beneath the highest yoke.

Unfortunately you cannot choose your masters.

Parenthesis About The Poet and The Child.

People often compare the poet to a child, for their innocence alone. I would compare them for their irresponsibility alone. Irresponsibility in everything except play.

When you come into this play with your human (moral) and man-made (social) laws, you will only break the game up and perhaps put an end to it.

By bringing in your conscience you will confuse ours (our creative one). "That isn't the way to play." But yes, this *is* the way to play.

Either the playing should be forbidden altogether (children's by us, ours by God), or else it shouldn't be interfered with.

What to you is "play" is to us the one thing that is serious.

Not even death will be more serious.

Whom To Judge, To Judge for What, and Who Should Judge.

A demon has lodged in a person. Do we judge the demon (the elemental)? Judge the fire that is burning down the house?

Judge me? For instance.

For what? For lack of conscience, will, strength: for *weakness*.

I shall answer with a question:

Why, out of all those who walk along the streets of Moscow and Paris, is it just me that it comes upon, and comes, outwardly, in such a way that I do not foam at the mouth, and I do not fall down on flat ground, and they do not take me off either to the hospital or to the police-station.

Why—if I *am* possessed—this external innocence (invisibility) of my possessed state (what is more innocent than writing poems!) and—if I *am* a criminal—this decorousness of my criminality? Why—if all this *is* so—is there no mark upon me? God brands the scoundrel, why doesn't God brand this scoundrel?

Why, on the contrary, instead of attempts to bring me to my senses, is there encouragement, and instead of a prison sentence—the affirmation that I am beyond jurisdiction?

—I am doing wicked work!

Society (a chorus of the seduced): No, you are doing *holy* work!

Why, even the most ideological government in the world shot a poet not for his poems (the essence) but for deeds which could have been done by anyone.

Why have I got to be my own doctor, tamer, guard?

Isn't it asking too much of me?

I'll answer with an answer:

Everything knowing is wittingly guilty. Because I am given a conscience (knowledge) I am, once for all—in all cases of contravening its laws, whether by weakness of will or strength of talent (what I call—a blow)—guilty.

Before God, not before men.

Who should judge? One who knows. Men do not know, indeed so little do they know, that they will beat from me the last of my knowledge. And if they judge, then, like that government mentioned above, it will not be for my poems but for my deeds (as if a poet had other deeds besides!), for the chance happenings of life, which are only consequences.

People judge me, for instance, for not sending my six-year-old son to school (to six hours on end of morning school!), not realizing that I don't send him precisely because I write poetry, like the following.

(From the poem to Byron)
Accomplished! He's alone between the sky and
water...
Here is a school for you, then, o you—hater of
schools!
And into the fated breast, pierced by a star,
Aeolus, king of fateful winds, is tearing his way in

—And I write this poetry precisely because I don't send him to school.

To praise me for my poetry and judge me for my son!

Oh, you—lickers of cream!

* * *

The teaching of literature in the secondary schools. They give the younger ones "The Drowned Man" and are surprised when they get frightened. They give the older ones Tatyana's letter and are surprised when they fall in love (shoot themselves). They put a bomb in their hands and are surprised when it explodes.

And—to finish with the subject of school:

If you like these poems, release the children (that is, meet the cost of your liking), or else—recognize that "liking" is not a measure of things and poems, is a measure not of things and poems but only of your own baseness (and the author's), that it is our common weakness before the elemental, for which at some hour, while still here upon earth, we shall be answerable.

Either release the children.

Or tear the poems out of the book.

* * *

I allow no one the right of judgment over a poet. Because nobody knows. Only the poets know, but they will not judge. And the priest will absolve.

The only judgment over a poet is self-judgment.

* * *

But apart from judgment, there is struggle: mine—with the element, yours—with me. Not to give in; I—to it, you—to me. That we be not seduced. Where shall I finally find the priest who will not absolve me of my poems?

Conclusion.

But—whether by command or by plea, by fear or by pity the elements overcome us, there are no reliable approaches— neither Christian, nor civic, nor any other kind. There is no approach to art, for it is a seizing. (While you are still approaching, it has already seized you.)

Example: Boris Pasternak in entire purity of heart, surrounding himself with all his materials, writes, copies from the life—right down to its inadvertencies!—*Lieutenant Schmidt*, and yet the main character in his work is—trees at a meeting. Over Pasternak's Square it is *they* that are the ringleaders. Whatever Pasternak might write, it is always the elements, not the characters, as in *Potemkin* it is the sea, not the sailors. Glory to Pasternak (Boris's human conscience) for the sailors, and glory to the sea, glory to his gift—for the sea, that insatiable sea for which all our gullets are too small and which can easily swallow us up (with all our stories and consciences).

Therefore, if you wish to serve God or man, if you have any wish to serve, to work for the good, then join the Salvation Army or something like that—and *give up poetry*.

But if your lyrical gift is indestructible, don't flatter yourself with the hope that you serve, even after completing a Hundred and Fifty Million. It is only your lyrical gift that has served you, tomorrow you will serve it, that is you'll be hurled by it leagues away from the goal you have set.

Vladimir Mayakovsky, who for twelve years on end served loyally and truly, body and soul—

> All my resounding poetic power.
> I'll give up to you, you attacking class!

ended more powerfully than with a lyrical poem—with a lyrical shot. For twelve years on end Mayakovsky the man killed in himself Mayakovsky the poet, in the thirteenth the poet arose and killed the man.

If there is in that life a suicide then it is not where people see it, and its duration was not that of the pressing of a trigger but—twelve years of life.

No imperial censor dealt with Pushkin as Vladimir Mayakovsky dealt with himself.

If there is in that life a suicide, then there is not one but two, and both are non-suicides, for the first is an act of valor, the second—a celebration. The overcoming of nature and the glorifying of nature.

He lived a human being and he died a poet.

To be a human being is more important, because more need-ed. The doctor and the priest are more needed than the poet be-cause they are at the deathbed, while we are not. Doctor and priest are humanly more important, all the rest are socially more important. (Whether the social is itself important is another ques-tion, which I shall have the right to answer only from an island.) Except for parasites, in all their various forms,–everyone is more important than we are.

And knowing this, having put my signature to this while of sound mind and in full possession of my faculties, I assert, no less in possession of my faculties and of sound mind, that I would not exchange my work for any other. Knowing the greater, I do the lesser, this is why there is no forgiveness for me. Only such as I will be held responsible at the Judgment Day of Conscience. But if there is a Judgment Day of the Word, at that I am inno-cent.

Translated by Angela Livingstone and Valentina Coe

NOTES ON THE SELECTIONS

The Life of Verse

First published in *Apollo*, No. 7 (1910). Translated from the text in N. Gumilev, *Sobranie sochinenii* (Washington: Kamkin, 1968), IV, 157-70. However, we have omitted "Part IV" of the essay, an obvious postscript, one page long, written to note the closing of the Symbolists' journal *The Scales* in 1909. "The Life of Verse" was Gumilev's first major essay on poetics. It is written from the point of view of an Acmeist, and published in a journal closely, but by no means exclusively, associated with Acmeism. On Acmeism and *Apollo* see: Denis Mickiewicz (ed.), "Toward a Definition of Acmeism," *Russian Language Journal*, East Lansing, Michigan (Supplementary Issue, Spring 1975) and Denis Mickiewicz, "*Apollo* and Modernist Poetics," in *The Silver Age of Russian Culture*, ed. C. and E. Proffer (Ann Arbor: Ardis, 1975), pp. 397-434.

"Dubinushka"—Or "Many songs have I heard," a very popular revolutionary song, written down by V.I. Bogdanov and revised by A.A. Olkhin. Often sung by Chaliapin before 1917.

"Aroused good feelings with his lyre"—A line from one of Pushkin's most famous lyric poems, "Exegi monumentum," popularly known as "A Monument" (1836). The poem is ambiguous enough that it has been used as a text by advocates of both "Art for Life" and "Art for Art's sake."

Saint John the Damascene (c. 675-749)—Gumilev may be alluding to his defense of ikon-worship or his revision of the Greek Orthodox Church's hymnbook.

Francois Coppée (1842-1908)—French poet and playwright, known as the *poète des humbles*, contributor to the *Parnasse contemporain* (1866).

Sully-Prudhomme (1839-1907)—French poet, Nobel Prize winner in 1901. In his later career his poetry favors the themes of the Parnassians.

Nikolai Nekrasov (1821-78)—Major poet and influential editor, known primarily for his civic verse and advocacy of reformist and radical causes.

Andrei Bely (1880-1934)—Poet, novelist, short-story writer, critic, scholar, theoritician, memoirist. One of the most prolific and talented writers of the Symbolist period. Best known in English for his novels, *Petersburg, Kotik Letaev,* and *The Silver Dove*. Gumilev's placing of Bely with these three poets is somewhat unexpected and no doubt polemical, but it is defensible. On Bely see: Samuel Cioran, *The Apocalyptic Symbolism of Andrei Bely* (The Hague, 1973) and J.D. Elsworth, *Andrei Bely* (Letchworth: Bradda Books, 1972).

Hérédia, José-Maria de (1842-1905)—French poet, one of the first Parnassians, known for perfection of technique and sharpness of image.

Apollon Maikov (1821-97)—An "aesthetic" poet, generally opposed to the "civic" poetry which dominated Russia in the mid-nineteenth century. His strongly imagistic verse would naturally appeal to an Acmeist such as Gumilev.

Hérodiade (1869)—A dramatic poem, in which the heroine symbolizes the cold, sterile solitude of the aesthetic life.

Oscar Wilde's words—In "The Critic as Artist, with some remarks upon the importance of discussing everything: a dialogue," *Intentions* (1891).

Semyon Nadson (1862-87)—A very popular poet, also inspired by civic themes, whose verse, according to D.S. Mirsky, "marks the low-water mark of Russian poetic technique."

"by irritation of a captive thought"—A line from Pushkin's poem.

Charles Asselineau (1820-74)—Critic and novelist known for elegant and erudite reviews, and his *L'Histoire du Sonnet*.

Pierre de Ronsard (1524?-85)—Best known for his *Sonnets pour Hélène* (1578).

François de Mainard (1582-1646)—Disciple of Malherbe's neoclassical teachings.

François de Malherbe (1555-1628)—Official court poet and neoclassical theoretician.

Turgenev's "A Quiet Backwater"—A short story (1854) in which the reading of Pushkin's poem (see next note) precipitates the suicide of Maria, who is hopelessly in love with a talented but frivolous man.

"The Upas Tree"—Or "Anchar" (1828), a lyric poem by Pushkin about a poison tree which destroys everything around it. A king sends a slave to get its resin for poison arrows—the slave does get the poison, but dies himself.

"The Poor Knight"—A poem by Pushkin (1829); the knight has a vision of the Virgin Mary, takes a vow to fight for her, but in his fanatic devotion to the female image, fails to pray to God. Therefore the devils try, successfully, to take him to Hell. Aglaia Epanchin in *The Idiot* (Part II, Chap 7) sees the knight as a man capable of blind faith in an ideal; she draws a parallel between the poem, Myshkin and Nastasya Fillipovna.

Sologub's "Night Dances" —"A Dramatic Tale in Three Acts," based on a fairytale from the famous Afanasiev collection. The role and power of the poet is a major theme. Fyodor Sologub (1863-1927) was a major Decadent, or Symbolist, poet and prose writer. Though best known abroad for his novels *The Petty Demon* and *The Created Legend,* connoisseurs of Russian poetry prize him for his elegant lyrics.

Lermontovian—Mikhail Lermontov (1814-41), Russia's most important Romantic poet. The "Young Poet" in Sologub's play uses the first stanza of Lermontov's celebrated lyric "I go out alone on the road" to distract beautiful princesses and escape a sleeping potion.

Valery Bryusov, "In the Crypt"—Bryusov (1873-1924) wrote this lyric in 1905, it was first published that year in his collection *Stephanos*. Bryusov was one of the most important and editorially powerful figures in the Russian Symbolist and Decadent movement. Poet, prose writer, translator and critic, he wrote prolifically, indeed some would say promiscuously. (He later became a Communist.) For further detail see Martin P. Rice, *Valery Bryusov and the Rise of Russian Sym-*

bolism (Ann Arbor, 1975).

Vyacheslav Ivanov (1866-1949)—Major Symbolist poet and theoretician, Russian classical scholar. From 1905 to 1911 the literary Wednesdays in his Tower apartment in St. Petersburg saw the cream of literary society gather. On Ivanov see: James West, *Russian Symbolism: A Study of Vyacheslav Ivanov* (London: Methuen, 1970).

"The Heliades" (Transparence)—A poem in Ivanov's second book (Moscow, 1904). The Harae, goddesses of the seasons, are associated with many deities, including Helios.

Eridanus—a mythical river with the Electrides Islands at its mouth.

Innokenty Annensky (1896-1909)—classicist, poet, teacher of Gumilev at the Tsarskoe Selo *gymnasium*. His most important book, *The Cypress Chest*, was published the year after his death. He translated Euripides and many other classical authors. See Vsevolod Setchkarev, *Studies in the Life and Works of Innokenty Annensky* (The Hague, 1963).

Blok's "Lady"—Alexander Blok (1880-1921) holds the often-disputed position of most important Russian Symbolist poet. The "Beautiful Lady," the Hagia Sophia, was his muse, also the title of an early collection of poems. See F.D. Reeve, *Alexander Blok: Between Image and Idea* (New York: Columbia, 1962).

Kuzmin's *Chimes of Love*—Moscow: Skorpion (1910), Mikhail Kuzmin's (1875-1936) musical pastorale in verse. Kuzmin was a composer, poet, dramatist, novelist, critic and translator; his essay "On Beautiful Clarity" (*Apollo*, 1910) is often seen as one of the first statements of Acmeist ideas. Translations into English include his homosexual novel *Wings: Prose and Poetry* (Ann Arbor, 1972) and the play *Venetian Madcaps* in *Russian Literature Triquarterly*, No. 7 (1973).

Tyutchevian night—Fyodor Tyutchev (1803-73) is often seen as a forerunner of the Symbolists, and in his work night is frequently a symbol of chaos and terror.

On the Nature of the Word

First published as a pamphlet, Kharkov: "Istoki," 1922. For details surrounding publication see Nadezhda Mandelstam, *Hope Abandoned* (New York, 1974), pp. 73-74.

"We have forgotten..." Gumilev—The epigraph, added by the publisher, consists of the final two stanzas of Gumilev's poem "The Word" (1921), and was omitted, by Mandelstam, from the 1928 publication of the essay.

Derzhavin or Simeon Polotsky—Gavrila Derzhavin (1743-1816) is generally regarded as the most important 18th-century Russian poet and Polotsky (1629-80) the most important 17th-century poet.

"quickening tempo of the historical process"—The violence and upheaval of wars and revolution in quick succession gave many Russian intellectuals the illusion that "history" was speeding up.

Bergson—Henri Bergson (1859-1941), French philosopher whose collected works were published in Russian between 1910 and 1914.

"theory of evolution...theory of progress"—Both Marxist literary theorists and the Russian Formalists used such terms in their writing.

author of *Boris Godunov*...Lyceum—Pushkin wrote the play in 1825; his earliest verse is called "Lyceum" verse after the school he attended in Tsarskoe Selo.

The *Lay of the Host of Igor*—anonymous epic "song" (usually dated 1187, though possibly it is many centuries younger), generally regarded as the greatest monument of Old Russian Literature.

Velimir Khlebnikov —pen-name of Viktor Vladimirovich Khlebnikov (1885-1922), eccentric genius of the Futurist movement, considered by most poets one of the most important figures in Russian poetry. For biography see V. Markov, *The Longer Poems of Velimir Khlebnikov* (Berkeley, 1962). For translations see V. Khlebnikov, *Snake Train: Poetry and Prose* (Ann Arbor: Ardis, 1976). Khlebnikov's tinkering with Slavic etymologies and creation of neologisms are central to his theories and his poetry, including that written in so-called "trans-sense language."

Saint Eulalia—Fragments of the "Cantilène de Sainte Eulalie" are among the earliest extant Vernacular French writings (end of the 9th century); until then Latin was the literary language.

"How can the heart fully express itself?"—from Tyutchev's most famous poem "Silentium" (1833), the idea of which is that one should hide one's thoughts and feelings in silence, because verbalization cheapens or simplifies them.

Futurism—The most raucous and revolutionary of modern Russian literary schools began, like Acmeism, around 1909. Mayakovsky and Khlebnikov were its major poets. Mandelstam and Mayakovsky are ideally antithetical figures, as the reader can see by following his reading of Mandelstam's essays with Mayakovsky's "How to Make Verse" (below). See also V. Markov, *Russian Futurism: A History* (Berkeley, 1968).

Imaginists—This group, of which Sergei Esenin was and is the best known, insisted on the supremacy of the metaphor in verse. The movement lasted, loosely, from 1919 to 1924. For details see Nils Nilsson, *The Russian Imaginists* (Stockholm, 1970) and Gordon McVay, *Esenin: A Life* (Ann Arbor: Ardis, 1976).

Chaadaev—Petr Chaadaev (1793?-1856), usually considered the grandfather of the "Westernizers" in Russia, was declared a lunatic and locked up for writing, in his *Philosophical Letters* (1830's), that Russia had no history and had produced nothing of value. Mandelstam has a separate essay devoted to him; see "Petr Chaadaev," in Osip Mandelstam, *The Complete Critical Prose and Letters* (Ann Arbor, 1976).

Rozanov—Vasily Rozanov (1856-1919), writer, critic and philosopher. Mirsky considers him among the greatest Russian writers, and he is currently undergoing a mild renaissance. His love of paradox and willingness to argue wildly differing points of view (under different names) led to charges of ideological hypocrisy. He was basically anti-positivist, mystical, Slavophile, and religious, but an immoralist whose writings on Christianity, the family and sex scandalized many readers. An English translation is V.V. Rozanov, *Solitaria* (tr. S.S. Kotliansky), New York, 1927. See also Renatto Poggioli, *Rozanov* (London: Bowes and Bower, 1962).

By the Cathedral Walls—1906.

Leontiev—Konstantin Leontiev (1831-91), diplomat, novelist, short-story writer, critic, but, mainly, a political writer, defender of (if not believer in) Orthodoxy and autocracy.

Gershenzon—Mikhail Gershenzon (1869-1925), an important conservative writer on philosophical, historical, and literary themes.

Nekrasov's famous line—The line which follows is the first line of a lyric poem describing how a young woman prostitutes herself to get money for her child's coffin.

Balmont—Konstantin Balmont (1867-1943), Decadent poet, celebrated for his alliterations and translations, including those of Poe's poems.

Dal's dictionary—Vladimir Dal [or Dahl] (1801-72), writer and lexicographer, whose four-volume *Dictionary of the Russian Language* (1861-68) is still a basic tool.

Pechenegs...Khazars—Fierce tribes who fought against the Russians in the South and East during medieval times.

"No longer do I begrudge..."—Last two lines of a free translation of Verlaine's "Pensées du Soir" (1887).

Euripides, Mallarmé, Le comte de Lisle—Annensky translated the Greek dramatist and both of the French poets—Stephane Mallarmé (1842-98) and Charles Le comte de Lisle (1818-94), the latter having especially strong Hellenic inspiration.

"Listen, a madman..."—Lines 3-8 of Annensky's poem "Nightmares" (pub. 1910). Gumilev called Annensky a great European poet—Gumilev was Annensky's pupil at the Tsarskoe Selo Lyceum, where Annensky was Director.

The Scales—(1904-1909), the most celebrated journal of the Russian Symbolists, it was modernistic in format and content, devoted solely to the arts.

"When the rapid river froze"—This is from Pushkin's narrative poem *The Gypsies* (1824), lines 198-201. The gypsy patriarch is telling Aleko the legend of Ovid ("the old man") having been exiled to the Caucasus.

"Anything transient is but a likeness"—*Alles Vergängliche/ist nur ein Gleichniss*—from the end of Goethe's *Faust*.

"correspondences"—A reference to Baudelaire's poem "Correspondances" (from *Flowers of Evil*), which was often alluded to as the metaphorical credo of the Symbolists, partly because of the phrase "forest of symbols" in line 3.

epoch known as Symbolism—Roughly, 1894-1909. The bibliography on Russian Symbolism is large. Begin with Georgette Donchin, *The Influence of French Symbolism on Russian Poetry* (The Hague, 1958) and Martin Rice, *Valery Briusov and the Rise of Russian Symbolism* (Ann Arbor: Ardis, 1975).

Jourdain—Monsieur Jourdain, title character of Moliere's *Le Bourgeois gentilhomme*, who is astonished he has been speaking prose all his life and didn't know it until a professor told him.

Organic school...Gorodetsky...Akhmatova, Narbut, Zenkevich—That is, Acmeism, or Adamism (see above, the first note to Gumilev's "The Life of Verse"). Sergei Gorodetsky (1884-1967) joined with Gumilev in organizing the Guild of Poets in 1911. Anna Akhmatova (1889-1966), Vladimir Narbut (1888-1944) and Mikhail Zenkevich (1891-1969) were all member-poets. Akhmatova is by far the most important of the poets named here. Her early books (*Beads*, 1919; *White Flock*, 1917; *Anno Domini MCMXXI*, 1922) were extraordinarily successful; in the 1920's she was silenced, but continued writing the rest of her life in spite of rarely being printed. Her admirers are divided into two camps—those who prefer her early love lyrics and those who praise her more complex later poems—including *Requiem* (1935-40) and *A Poem without a Hero* (1940-42). Translations of her poems can be found in *Russian Literature Triquarterly*, No. 1 (1971) and No. 9 (1974), and Walter Arndt, ed., *Selected Poetry of Anna Akhmatova* (Ann Arbor: Ardis, 1976); Stanley Kunitz and Max Hayward, ed. and trans. *Poems of Akhmatova* (New York, 1974). On her life and works see Sam Driver, *Anna Akhmatova* (New York: Twayne, 1972).

Chénier—André Chénier (1762-94), French poet. See also Osip Mandelstam, "Remarks on Chénier," in *The Complete Critical Prose and Letters*.

Odoevsky...Novalis—V.F. Odoevsky (1803-69), short-story writer greatly influenced by German Romantics such as philosopher Friedrich Schelling—whose ideas influenced E.T.A. Hoffmann (1776-1822) and Novalis (pseudonym of Friedrich von Hardenberg, 1772-1801), poet and novelist.

men of the 60's read...Buckle—The Russian radical social writers of the 1860's (N.G. Chernyshevsky, N. Dobrolyubov, etc.) approved of English historian Henry Thomas Buckle's "scientific" view that history was a march of progress of human improvement.

"The rational abyss of the Gothic soul"—Line 10 of Mandelstam's poem "Notre Dame" (1912).

Salieri—Antonio Salieri (1750-1825), Italian composer, made a symbol of cold, mathematical, uninspired creativity by Pushkin in his play *Mozart and Salieri* (1830). See Nadezhda Mandelstam's *Mozart and Salieri: An Essay on the Poetry of Osip Mandelstam* (Ann Arbor: Ardis, 1973).

On the Addressee

First published in *Apollon*, No. 2 (1913), 49-54. It was written when Mandelstam was twenty-one.

"to the shores...resonant oaks"—The two closing lines of Pushkin's 20-line lyric "The Poet" (1827). The poet is silent and insignificant until called to the "sacrifice of Apollo," but when the divine word touches him his soul awakens like an eagle.

"God's bird"—In Pushkin's narrative-dramatic poem *The Gypsies* (1824), there is an interpolated song which is really an extended comparison: the free bird, knowing no trouble, is inspired to sing by God, and flies away to warm climes in the fall—like the hero of *The Gypsies*, Aleko. There is no parallel with poets, although the imagery is related to that in "The Poet."

François Villon—(1431-1463?) French murderer and poet, to whom Mandelstam devoted a whole essay later. See *The Complete Critical Prose*. One of Villon's poems is addressed: "Frères, humains qui aprés nous vivez."

"My gift is poor"...Baratynsky—Evgeny Baratynsky (1800-1844), a major poet of the Romantic period, wrote this lyric in 1828.

"I know no wisdom.." —Balmont's poem was published in 1902.

"I am a sudden outburst"—Lines 5-6 of Balmont's egocentric poem "Snake's Eye" (1901).

Pushkin's quarrel with the..."mob"—In a series of poems, particularly "The Poet and the Mob" (1829), Pushkin portrays the mob as a mob, the poet as superior, born not for mundane concerns but "for inspiration, sweet sounds and prayers."

"Here we are, all ears"—A free translation of the last line of the mob's second speech in "The Poet and the Mob."

"A great poet...your obligation"—An extremely famous couplet (lines 170-71) from Nikolai Nekrasov's poem "The Poet and the Citizen" (1856), which in many ways was a polemic with Pushkin's views on the poet (expressed in the poems which Mandelstam is discussing here).

The Shaken Tripod

First published as a pamphlet, St. Petersburg: "Epokha," 1922. Reprinted in *Mosty*, IX (1962), 3-10.

Khodasevich presented this essay on February 13, 1921 in the Dom literatorov in Petrograd during the so-called "Pushkinskie dni" ["Pushkin Days"] which were to mark the eighty-fourth anniversary of Pushkin's death. Much of what Khodasevich said that day remains true, and much is already an anachronism. The views presented here, however, retain their intrinsic interest not so much for their literary insight into Pushkin and his poetry, but rather as a document of Russian intellectual history. The revolution of 1917 and the years of civil war that followed did, indeed, as Khodasevich notes, create a certain void between the Russia of Pushkin and the new Soviet reality. Khodasevich's essay can thus be seen as a jeremiad of sorts that spiritually connects the Silver Age of Russian poetry with her Golden Age, and voices an anguished cry—indeed, a *plach'*—at the loss of communication between generations of Russian poets, while at the same time pointing to the intimate spiritual affinity that bound the poets of Khodasevich's circle to the best traditions of Russian poetry as represented by Pushkin.

In translating this essay, I have tried to follow as closely as possible the language of Khodasevich, though in several instances, for the sake of clarity, I have opted to sacrifice the specific in order to preserve the meaning and the spirit of the general. *[Translator's Note]*

The Bronze Horseman—Pushkin's best narrative poem, written in 1833. A literal translation maybe found in J. Fennell (ed.), *Pushkin* (Baltimore: Penguin Books, 1964), a verse translation in Walter Arndt (ed.), *Pushkin Threefold* (New York: Dutton, 1972).

Mickiewicz—Adam Mickiewicz (1798-1855), the greatest Polish poet, whose devastating description of Russia (*Dziady*, 1832) was countered by the introductory ode in *The Bronze Horseman*. See W. Lednicki, *Pushkin's Bronze Horseman* (Berkeley, 1955).

Gershenzon's book—M.O. Gershenzon, *The Wisdom of Pushkin* (Moscow, 1919), after more than half a century is still one of the most interesting studies of the poet.

1905—That is, the "first Russian Revolution," which occurred that year.

Pisarev "abolished" Pushkin—Dmitri Pisarev (1840-68), a young nihilist critic wrote a long essay on Pushkin and Belinsky (1865) attacking Vissarion Belinsky's "idealistic" interpretations of Pushkin and reducing Pushkin to an empty dandy with a glossy style. During the second half of the 19th century, Pushkin's reputation was low in many circles, particularly where utilitarian ideas and materialistic thinking dominated. It was, in fact, this camp which eventually emerged victorious in the 1917 October Revolution.

"first eclipse...second"—Khodasevich assumed that Marxist ideology was not compatible with appreciation of Pushkin. As it turned out, Bolshevism led not to the eclipse of Pushkin, but to the vulgarization of him in mountains of secondary literature and anniversary claptrap.

Dahl's dictionary—Dates from the 1860s. See index for Dahl [Dal].

"And long shall I remain liked by the people"—A line from Pushkin's poem "Exegi Monumentum" (1836). For a translation see Fennel, *op. cit.*, p. 75. In Gershenzon's interpretation of the poem (in *The Wisdom of Pushkin*), Pushkin's remarks on "the people" are ironic—the common people love the poet for the wrong reasons.

"the crowd spits at the altar of the poet...shakes his tripod in 'childlike playfulness"—These phrases, including the tripod of Khodasevich's title, are taken from Pushkin's sonnet "To the Poet" (1830). Pushkin urges the poet not to value the love of the people, arguing that the poet is a tsar whose own judgment is above all else. The last three lines:

> Are you satisfied? Then let the crowd [mob] curse it
> And spit on the altar where your fire burns,
> And in childlike playfulness shake your tripod.

"**And from the fates there's no protection**"—The last line of Pushkin's *The Gypsies*.

On the Mission of the Poet

This essay was first a talk given at the House of Writers (Dom literatorov), February 13, 1921—the same evening as Khodasevich's "The Shaken Tripod." First published in *Vestnik literatury*, No. 3 (27), 1921.

"**...the ship of modernity**"—In the Futurists' manifesto "A Slap in the Face of Public Taste" (1912), Mayakovsky and others demanded Pushkin and other "dead" artists of the past be rejected, thrown overboard from the ship of modernity. For a full translation of the document see *Russian Literature Triquarterly*, No. 12 (1975), 179-80.

"**What is a poet?**"—For a detailed analysis of Blok's view of the poet, contrasted to the views of Pushkin and other poets, see Victor Erlich, *The Double Image* (Yale University Press).

agonizes lonely Salieri—In Scene Two of Pushkin's one-act play *Mozart and Salieri*. For a verse translation, see A.S. Pushkin, *Little Tragedies*, tr. E. Kayden (Yellow Springs, Ohio: Antioch University Press, 1965). For a literal prose translation see John Fennell, *op. cit.*, pp. 207-22.

Count Beckendorff, Timkovsky, Bulgarin—All officials, civil or literary, who hounded Pushkin during his lifetime.

"**Among the worthless children...**"—From Pushkin's "The Poet."

"**The cares of the bustling world**"—Also from "The Poet."

"**He runs, frantic and grim...**"—Also from "The Poet."

"**primordial chaos**"—From Fyodor Tyutchev's poem "Of what do you sing, evening wind" (1836).

"**Inspiration**," said Pushkin—In the original this is followed by one other sentence: "Inspiration is necessary in geometry as it is in poetry"; see *The Critical Prose of Alexander Pushkin* (Bloomington: Indiana University Press, 1969), p. 52.

The term "rabble"—This and the following four paragraphs all allude to Pushkin's poem "The Poet and the Mob."

"**It's small grief to me...**"—Pushkin's "From Pindemonte" (1836).

"**To be/Accountable to no man...**"—"From Pindemonte."

"Love and secret freedom..."—From Pushkin's "To N. Ya. Plyuskovaya" (1819).

Fet—Poet A.A. Fet (1820-92) in his "To a Pseudo-poet" (1867), directed at the civic poet Nikolai Nekrasov.

Belinsky drooled—Vissarion Belinsky (1811-1848), the most famous Russian critic, wrote very extensively on Pushkin, but his sociological turn of mind was naturally deplored by esthetes such as Blok.

"An elevating Illusion..."—From Pushkin's poem "The Hero" (1831).

Pisarev—See the note on Pisarev's "Pushkin and Belinsky" above, page 193.

Schiller—F. Schiller in his tragedy *Don Carlos*, Act V, Scene 9.

d'Anthès—d'Anthès killed Pushkin in a duel in 1837.

"It's time, my friend, it's time!"—The first line of a famous Pushkin lyric (1834).

Let those bureaucrats...—Censorship and other official controls on literature had already become quite harsh in the years since the 1917 Revolution.

Some Statements

First published in *Sovremennik*, No. 1 (Moscow, 1922); translated from Boris Pasternak, *Stikhi: 1936-59* (Ann Arbor, 1961), 152-55. Originally, Pasternak planned to call this piece "Quintessence"

Swinburne...Chastelard—Swinburne wrote a trilogy of plays about Mary Stuart; the first play of the trilogy was *Chastelard* (1865), which Pasternak translated. According to Pasternak's "Autobiographical Sketch" he lost the translation in 1914 along with other books and manuscripts during anti-German riots in Moscow (Pasternak happened to be tutor in a German household which was destroyed.)

Châtelard was a somewhat unbalanced young poet whose unseemly assaults on Mary's chambers led to his execution in 1563.

Mary herself did write poetry, in French, to Ronsard among others.

Yelabuga blizzard knew Scottish—That is, a Russian poet writing in a storm in the town of Yelabuga (where some 30 years later Tsetaeva would hang herself) could translate Swinburne.

from *A Safe Conduct*

First published in *Zvezda*, Book 8 (1929) and *Krasnaia nov'*, Books 4,5,6 (1931). Translated from Pasternak, *Proza 1915-58* (Ann Arbor, 1961), pp. 213-216, 233-35, 241-44, 281-82.

For a complete translation of this autobiographical work see: B. Pasternak, *Prose and Poems* (London: Ernest Benn Ltd., 1959), 11-128.

Musaget—A publishing house which favored the Symbolists.

Marburg...Cohen, Natorp—Pasternak studied in Marburg before World War I began; Hermann Cohen and Paul Natorp were among his teachers. Bernard Natorp was one of the philosophers studied.

Tolstois and Wedekinds—Leo Tolstoi (1828-1910) wrote a long story on the subject of destructive illicit sex called *The Kreutzer Sonata* (1890). Frank Wedekind (1864-1918), German dramatist, portrayed society in lurid light in his *Pandora's Box* (1904), the heroine of which is a demonic Lulu.

Tristan—*Tristan and Iseult*, a medieval cycle of tales, like *Romeo and Juliet* one of the archetypical love stories.

Over the Barriers—Pasternak's second collection of poems (1917).

Esenin—Sergei Esenin (1895-1925), popular "peasant" poet.

My Sister Life—Pasternak's third, and greatest, book of poetry (published in 1922).

from *Notes of a Translator*

Section I here first appeared as "Notes of a Translator," *Znamia*, Books 1-2 (1944). Section II here first appeared as "My New Translations," *Ogonek*, No. 47 (1942); and Section III as "Notes to Translations of Shakespeare's Tragedies," *Literaturnaia Moskva*, Book I (1956). Translations of the excerpts from these three pieces here are made from B. Pasternak, *Stikhi 1936-59* (Ann Arbor: University of Michigan Press, 1961), pp. 183-85, 192, 193-94, 194-95.

Lermontov's...Anglomania—The two Russian poets were strongly influenced by English Romantics, especially Byron, both in their lyrics and their longer narrative poems.

Balmont translation—Balmont translated Shelley very freely, so freely that some readers referred to the Balmont versions of Shelley as "Shellmont." Pasternak, both in theory and in his own practice favored very free translation.

Zhukovsky—Vasily Zhukovsky (1783-1852), one of the first important Russian poets, was known mainly as a translator. Most of his versions were heavily reworked and bore little literal resemblance to the originals—beginning the practice which has dominated Russian translations of poetry to this day.

Verhaeren and Rilke—Emile Verhaeren (1855-1916), Belgian poet and Rainier Maria Rilke (1875-1926), Austrian poet, were among the favored writers of the Russian Symbolists—and Rilke was especially important for Pasternak and Tsvetaeva later.

Voltaire and Tolstoi—Voltaire and Leo Tolstoi were among the famous detractors of Shakespeare. See Voltaire's 1776 *Lettre* to the French Academy and Tolstoi's "Shakespeare and the Drama" (1903-1906).

How is Verse Made?

First published by sections in newspapers and journals (1926) from *Leningrad Pravda* to *Star of the East* (Tbilisi, Georgia). Translated from V. Maiakovskii, *Polnoe sobranie sochinenii* (M. 1959), XII, 81-117.

the Formalists—A group of Russian critics in the teens and twenties who sought to analyze literary "structures" scientifically, describing devices like anatomists.

as Onegin loved Tatyana—Onegin and Tatyana are the hero and heroine of Pushkin's *Eugene Onegin.*

Pushkin's "disenchanted lorgnette"—The epithet is from *Eugene Onegin.*

"my uncle is of most honest principles"—The first line of *Eugene Onegin.*

Shengeli's rules—G.A. Shengeli (1894-1956), minor poet and translator, wrote a variety of handbooks including *How to Write Essays, Poems, and Stories* (M. 1926), and one book (in 1927) attacking Mayakovsky.

M. Brodovsky, Grech—M. Brodovsky's *Guide to Versification* (1907); Nikolai Grech's *Textbook of Russian Literature* (1820).

N. Abramov—His *Complete Dictionary of Russian Rhymes* (1912) was, from Mayakovsky's point of view, very incomplete.

Gippius—A garbled citation from Zinaida Gippius's poem "Now" ("Seichas").

Kirillov—Opening stanza of "To the Sailors" by V.T. Kirillov (1889-1943). A "Smithy" poet, singer of a machine-tooled future (approved by Mayakovsky) but in old forms (not approved).

"Keep the revolutionary step"—From Blok's narrative poem "The Twelve" (1918).

Mayakovsky—The first line of Mayakovsky's poem "Left March."

"untiring enemy is always alert"—A line from Blok's "The Twelve."

"Gobble your pineapple"—A 1917 Mayakovsky poem (2 lines in Russian).

Chastushki—A popular rhymed jingle or song, originally folkloric, formally very diversified.

The fellow-travellers—Writers who went along with the Revolution, though not Party members or ideologues.

"I go out alone into the road"—The first line of a famous and (through repetition) hackneyed lyric by Lermontov (1841).

Yudenich—A White General.

Demyan Bedny—Bedny (1883-1945) was a Party poet who wrote in variations of folk genres, updating fables and fairytales for propaganda purposes.

Kruchenykh—Alexei Kruchenykh (1886-1968), along with Mayakovsky (but far less talented), a Futurist poet.

N.O.T.—Russian initials for the "Scientific Organization of Labor" bureau.

a cloud in trousers—Mayakovsky's most famous long poem is entitled *A Cloud in Trousers* (1914-15). For a translation see Pat Blake and Max

Hayward (eds.) *The Bedbug and Selected Poetry* (Bloomington: Indiana University Press, 1975).

Pasternak's brilliant quatrain—Mayakovsky slightly alters the first quatrain of Pasternak's "Marburg" (1917).

"To Sergei Esenin"—The poem was written in early 1926, published in April.

In the early morning of Dec. 28, 1925 Esenin hanged himself in a Leningrad hotel. Roughly twenty-four hours before this he had written his last poem—in blood from his arm. A literal translation follows:

Goodbye, my friend, goodbye.
My dear, you are in my heart.
Predestined separation
Promises a future meeting.

Goodbye, my friend, without handshake and words,
Do not grieve and sadden your brow,—
In this life there's nothing new in dying,
But nor, of course, is living any newer.

This was an end to a very disorderly and "colorful" life which included marriage to Isadora Duncan, political turnabouts, and frequent anti-social behavior. But Esenin was, and is, an extremely popular poet, a worthy rival of Mayakovsky in this respect. For detail see Gordon McVay, *Esenin: A Life* (Ann Arbor: Ardis, 1976).

Klyuev—Nikolai Klyuev (1887?-1937), gay Russian "peasant" poet, Esenin's mentor at one time.

Gorky—Maxim Gorky (1868-1936), the well-known prose writer and apologist.

"My dear, dear funny fool..."—A line from Esenin's long poem *Sorokoust* (1920).

"A Bolshevik is what I am"—From Esenin's poem "Jordan Dove" (1918).

Esenin left for America—In 1922-23 Esenin visited the United States with Isadora Duncan.

VAPP—Acronym of the All-Union Association of Proletarian Writers, a pro-revolutionary group.

LEF...Aseev—Left Front of the Arts, the militantly pro-revolutionary group (and journal) of Mayakovsky. Poet Nikolai Aseev (1889-1963) was another member.

The morning papers carried his last lines—Apparently because of the newspapers it was widely believed that Esenin slashed his wrist, wrote the poem cited above, and then hanged himself all on the same night. But this is not true. (See McVay, *op. cit.*)

Bezymensky—Alexander Bezymensky (1898-1973), a Party, proletarian poet, wrote a poem called "An Encounter with Esenin."

Zharov—A quote from A. Zharov's poem "On Esenin's Coffin" (1926).

Kogan—P.S. Kogan, a literary critic, wrote several panegyrical pieces after Esenin's suicide.

six (!) booklets—Kruchenykh published a steady series of brochures about Esenin in 1926.

The Week by Libedinsky—A short novel (1922) by Yury Libedinsky (1898-1959) showing ruling Communists in a favorable light.

the collection *Petals*—A 1924 collection of writings by workers.

Radimov's piglets—An allusion to A. Radimov's poem "Herd of Pigs"; Mayakovsky also made fun of him for using archaic forms for modern poems.

"Victims you fell..."—A line from a popular revolutionary song ("Funeral March").

"We'll defeat the decadent order"—A popular revolutionary song from the 1870's by P.L. Lavrov.

"The steed fell on the battlefield"—A line from Glinka's opera *Ivan Susanin.*

Sobinovs—L.V. Sobinov, an opera singer who sang about Esenin's death at memorial gatherings.

Doronin—I.I. Doronin wrote a long poem called *The Iron Ploughman* (1926).

Utkin—From I.P. Utkin's poem "The Burial Mound" (1926).

"We are veterans..."—Imprecise quote of a Bryusov translation of a Verhaeren poem.

War and the World—A long poem by Mayakovsky, the title of which, in Russian, is a homonym for *War and Peace.*

Selvinsky's—Ilya Selvinsky (1899-1968), a well known Constructivist poet.

Balmont: "I'm a wandering wind..."—In the original of Balmont's "Snow Flowers" there is a ludicrously heavy alliteration of "v" and "e."

Alexei Tolstoy—(1817-1875), poet and dramatist. His ballad "Vasily Shibanov" is the source of these lines.

as Pushkin intended—In Pushkin's tragedy *Boris Godunov* the Pretender says these words.

Art in the Light of Conscience

First published in *Sovremennye Zapiski,* Vol. L (Paris, 1932), pp. 305-26; Vol. LI (1932), pp. 251-64. The unfinished work is part of a book which Tsvetaeva did not complete. In an article devoted to the piece ["Tsvetaeva's *Art in the Light of Conscience,*" *Russian Literature Triquarterly,* No. 11 (1975), pp. 363-78], Angela Livingstone writes:

Given the abrupt and somewhat cryptic style of even her finished pieces of prose, it is hard to be absolutely sure where the unfinished quality shows in this piece. But it is there in the occasional jotting down of verbless phrases, like headings, pointing to what comes next, and in the way a sentence containing an idea is sometimes placed in isolation between two paragraphs as if to be developed later on, as well as in many passages that seem to require elaboration.

A peculiarity of Tsvetaeva's prose is that she writes as if in mid-utterance to someone.

"There is an ecstasy in battle..."—This line and the succeeding ones in this section of Tsvetaeva's essay come from Pushkin's *The Feast during the Plague* (1830), written when Pushkin was quarantined on his estate Boldino during a cholera "plague." It is basically a translation of Act I, Scene 4, John Wilson's *The City of the Plague* (1816). For a translation "back" see A. Pushkin, *Little Tragedies*, op. cit., pp. 83-96. Pushkin does add two songs to the text. The context: a group of revellers carouses in defiance of Death. The "chairman" or master of ceremonies is named Walsingham; one of the songs Pushkin adds is given to Walsingham—a hymn in honor of the Plague. It is ended by the appearance of a Priest who rebukes Walsingham for acting this way when his mother and wife were just recently killed by the plague. He refuses to end the feast, and is left brooding.

Bedlams and Charentons—Insane asylums in England and France.

Werther—*The Sorrows of Young Werther* (1774), by writing which Goethe is supposed to have found a way to bear the suffering of loving a woman who belonged to another. Because his hero commits sublimative suicide.

"President"—That is, the "chairman" of the feast, Walsingham.

"Apollonian" principle—That is, the common view of Pushkin as clear, uncomplicated and spontaneous.

Pugachov, Mazeppa, Peter—Peasant rebel Pugachov, real-life hero of Pushkin's novel *The Captain's Daughter*; Ukrainian hetman Mazeppa, real-life hero of his poem *Poltava*; Peter the Great—who is in several of Pushkin's works.

"of the free element"—Pushkin's poem "To the Sea" (1824) begins: "Farewell, free element!"

1830. Boldino—Date and place where *The Feast During the Plague* was written.

Tolstoi's crusade—In *What is Art* (1898) and other later writings, Tolstoi rejected most of his own works and those of most generally acclaimed writers and artists. He argued that good art should convey ordinary feelings, simple morals, and the religious perception in which he believed. He took up cobbling to help justify his existence—by doing something truly useful.

Childhood and *Boyhood*—The first two parts of Tolstoi's autobiographical trilogy (1852, 1854).

Karl-August—Goethe became a minister in Weimar for the Duke Karl-August.

Blok's "music of the revolution"—Blok reported that the noise, hum or music of the Revolution was resounding in his ears when he wrote "The Twelve" in early 1918.

Z.G.—Zinaida Gippius, who loathed "The Twelve" for its apparent praise of the Revolution.

Vozdvizhenka..."Katka!"—A street in Moscow. Katka is a bourgeoise character in "The Twelve" who is shot dead by a Red Guardsman.

Dead Souls—Nikolai Gogol (1809-52), who had a sharp nose, burned Part II of his novel *Dead Souls* in 1852, believing that despite his efforts he had failed to write a book of high spiritual and artistic worth. For detail see the *Letters of Nikolai Gogol*, ed. and tr. C.R. Proffer (Ann Arbor: University of Michigan Press, 1967).

Art without novitiate—In Russian, a play on words of the sort very frequent in this essay: *isskusstvo bez iskusa*. (*Iskus* means "novitiate," "ordeal," "test," "probation.")

my...daughter—Ariadna Tsvetaeva (1912-1975) did not have the talent her mother imagined.

Alfred de Vigny (1797-1843)—French Romantic poet, one of Tsvetaeva's numerous writer-heroes.

Hölderlin—Friedrich Hölderlin (1770-1843), German poet, author of highly spiritual verse.

Nekrasov the citizen—See note on Nekrasov's poem "The Poet and the Citizen," above, p. 192.

Bazarovism—Beliefs in keeping with the anti-romantic, materialistic views of Bazarov, hero of Turgenev's novel *Fathers and Sons* (1862).

Artsybashev's Sanin—Mikhail Artsybashev (1878-1927) wrote a scandalous novel called *Sanin* (1907) in which the hero applies Nietzscheanism to sex.

"She took the faded pages"—From Fyodor Tyutchev's poem "She was sitting on the floor" (1858).

"Molodets"—"The Swain," an epic, stylized as a folk epic, by Tsvetaeva (1924).

or a wizard—my forebear—In Russian *libo chura: prashchura*. The sound-play cannot be reproduced in translation; the word *chura*, nominative *chur*, is also very hard to translate. It means "limit," "circle," and is generally used in magical contexts. Unless Tsvetaeva means that she serves a magical limit, she appears to be inventing a use or meaning for this word which we have hopefully rendered by the personification "wizard" because of the following notion (personal) of "ancestor." [*Translator's note*]

brother, Jules Goncourt—Edmond and Jules Goncourt (1822-96, 1830-70) carried artistic sensibility to the point of hyperesthesia. Jules died of syphilis, not excessive sensitivity, as his brother, and Tsvetaeva, thought.

Craft of *Mra*—A Tsvetaeva neologism based on the words for death and darkness.

Et tout le rest...—A slight misquotation of a line from Paul Verlaine's "Art poètique" (1874).

"And you send reply"—From Pushkin's lyric "Echo" (1832).

Nicht Vorhanden—German, "not present" (containing the word "hand").

"Who called me;"—In Goethe's *Faust*, Part I, the earth-spirit summoned by Faust asks this ("Wer ruft mir?").

Artistic-vulneral—We have invented this word (looking to the Latin *vulnus* [wound] to translate the Russian *bolevoi*, an adjective formed from *bol'* (pain), and meaning "having to do with pain" rather than "painful." [*Translator's note*]

unhappy crowned contemplator—Emperor Charles V of Austria who abdicated in 1830, complaining he couldn't make a few watches that kept the same time, let alone make all people think alike.

all my Russian works—Tsvetaeva apparently means works written using folk stylization.

Pushkin feared Nicholas...Pugachov—Tsar Nicholas I, who was Pushkin's personal censor—and watchdog. Pushkin wrote extensively on Peter the Great and on the peasant rebel Pugachov.

Grishka Optrepev—Monk, the False Pretender who won the Russian throne in 1605-1606, is a character in Pushkin's *Boris Godunov*.

a Corsican—That is, a Napoleon.

ship of Odysseus...wax—In Homer's *Odyssey* (12.39, 184) the Sirens, who charm sailors onto the rocks, are thwarted by Odysseus—he is lashed to a mast, and his sailors' ears are stuffed with wax.

Mayakovsky...Volunteer leader...Crimea—Mayakovsky devoted much of his poetic energy to defending the Revolution. In spite of her quite different attitude, Tsvetaeva made Mayakovsky one of her own heroes, devoting a cycle of poems to him, and writing an essay called "Epic and Lyric in Contemporary Russia: Mayakovsky and Pasternak" (translated in *Russian Literature Triquarterly*, No. 13 (1975), pp. 519-42.

General Vrangel was a White Army leader particularly hated by the Reds. In Mayakovsky's long poem *It's Good!* (1927) he describes Vrangel's ignominious flight from Russia (section 16, lines 2440 ff.). Neither of Mayakovsky's two poems entitled "Crimea" mention Vrangel.

the content of the possessed condition—This sentence cannot be exactly translated because of typical and, here, extreme, use of word-play, play upon the root syllables of similar words. In Russian it is: *Iskusstvo yest' to, cherez chto stikhiia derzhit—i oderzhivaet; i sredstvo derzhaviia (nas—stikhiiami), a ne samoderzhavie, sostoianie oderzhimosti, ne soderzhanie oderzhimosti.* Thus the words we have translated by "holds," "overpowers," "the holding," "autarchy," "being possessed," "content," and "possessed condition"—all have as their root syllable the syllable *—derzh—* (hold). [*Translator's note*]

shot a poet—Gumilev was executed by the Cheka in 1921.

the poem to Byron—Tsvetaeva's "I've left the clime of misty Albion" (1918).

"The Drowned Man"—By Pushkin (1828).

Tatyana's letter—Her letter to Onegin in Pushkin's *Eugene Onegin*, in which she confesses her love.

Lieutenant Schmidt—A long poem by Pasternak (1926-27) about a Revolutionary sailor on the Black Sea in 1905.

Potemkin—A poem (written 1925) about the 1905 mutiny of the battleship Potemkin; later used as a section called "Mutiny at Sea" in his long poem *The Year 1905*.

150,000,000—The title of a poem by Mayakovsky (1919-20).

"all my resounding poetic power"—From Mayakovsky's long poem *Vladimir Ilych Lenin* (1924).

ended...with a lyrical shot—Mayakovsky shot himself to death in 1930.

no Imperial censor—An allusion to the fact that Tsar Nicholas I was Pushkin's censor.